A book for
Family Reading

YOU SANK MY BOAT!

A book for
Family Reading

YOU SANK MY BOAT!

Fifty-two stories that teach biblical truths

Jim Cromarty

EVANGELICAL PRESS

EVANGELICAL PRESS
Faverdale North Industrial Estate, Darlington, DL3 0PH, England

Evangelical Press USA
P. O. Box 84, Auburn, MA 01501, USA

e-mail: sales@evangelical-press.org

web: www.evangelical-press.org

First published 1999

British Library Cataloguing in Publication Data available

ISBN 0 85234 432 5

Printed and bound in Great Britain by Creative Print & Design Wales, Ebbw Vale.

This book is dedicated to all parents who take seriously
the words of our God:

'Hear, O Israel: The LORD our God, the LORD is one! You shall love the LORD your God with all your heart, with all your soul, and with all your strength. And these words which I command you today shall be in your heart. You shall teach them diligently to your children, and shall talk of them when you sit in your house, when you walk by the way, when you lie down, and when you rise up...' (Deuteronomy 6:4-7).

Contents

Preface

Once again we have a book of stories with a suggested Bible reading and text of Scripture that families can use in their daily family worship. Others may simply read the chapters in order to understand more of the eternal God who loved his people and gave his only begotten Son to live and die as their substitute, thus providing a sure way of salvation to all who believe in him.

In our busy world where time is always a short commodity, Christian parents must make the time to gather their families around the Word of God and glorify his wondrous name. Family worship is a sure way of instructing your precious family in the truths of Scripture and pointing them to Christ. It is a wonderful witness to the young people that you love Christ and take the issues of life and death very seriously. Many times we hear or read of Christians thanking their faithful parents for having taken the time each day to uphold them before the throne of grace and encourage them to flee to Christ from the wrath to come. May our children say the same of us.

Jim Cromarty

It's time to grow up!

Read
• • • • • • • • • • • • • • • • • • •
Hebrews 5:12 - 6:3

'Brethren, do not be children in understanding; however, in malice be babes, but in understanding be mature' (1 Corinthians 14:20).

Many years ago I was a baby, but over the years I have grown to maturity. Once I lived on milk and probably spent a lot of time crying and making baby noises. However, now I eat meat, fruit and vegetables and speak in a language that others can understand. Growing up took a long time for me and it involved many years at school as well as the time I spent learning how to get on well with other people.

Our dog, Wags, was the smallest in the litter. When we brought him home he drank milk and that was about all. Today he has grown into a small but well-built dog. He still likes his milk, but now eats meat, apple, cheese, dog biscuits, chocolate — and anything else that he happens to see. Wags has grown up!

A new area of land was developed in Wingham some years ago and a lot of builders began building homes for people who had purchased a plot of land. Some houses were of only one storey; others had two storeys; some were of brick, some timber — they were all different, but they reached the stage where their owners moved in and

11

turned their houses into homes. However, there was one builder who completed the cement flooring and that was where he finished. I guess the owners had run out of money. And now the cement flooring is still there, but that is all. I have been told, however, that someone is buying the plot of land and expects to complete the building.

In this world people, animals, plants and buildings start in a small way and then usually grow to maturity. If they remain small we know that something is wrong and we are disappointed when this happens.

Today's Bible reading speaks of Christians who do not grow. These are the people who know they are sinners and, turning to Christ, trust their salvation to him. But that is as far as they go. They don't read much of their Bibles, and when they do they spend their time reading and rereading the wonderful story of what Christ has done for them. However, they never get down to a real study of all the great truths taught in the Bible. They remain spiritual babies.

Of course the writer to the Hebrews was speaking to the Jews who loved the old ways and found it difficult to put them all aside, especially as many still believed that they had to add good works to their faith in order to be saved. The readers of the letter to the Hebrews had to understand that many of the old ways now had no value in salvation. Nor was there any use spending more time going over the basic principles of the Christian faith. They had to move on to the great doctrines. It was time to grow up. They were acting like babies who depended upon milk for food and even though they were adults they still wanted only to drink milk. What they needed was a good plate of solid spiritual food!

12

Sometimes I speak to people who have been professing Christians for many years, but when we start talking about the significance of the Lord's Supper, they show they don't really understand what they are doing when they sit at the Lord's Table. If the discussion gets around to what happens when a person dies, again they are not sure; and if you mention the wonderful doctrine of election they throw up their hands and say, 'Don't confuse me with those doctrines. They are for the theologians. I just love Christ and that's all that matters.'

In my previous books a lot of what I wrote has been spiritual milk. Now I want to give you some solid food that will help you to grow spiritually. I'm going to write about hell and heaven, regeneration, sanctification, justification and the hard-to-understand doctrines of election and predestination. I pray that you will come to the end of this book with a better understanding of these wonderful truths that will cause you to love and admire God more and more. Don't be frightened by some strange words. Learn what they mean and then don't be afraid to start using them yourself. That will help you to become a mature, grown-up, Christian.

I have a computer and am faced by very strange words. However, this is the computer language that all users need to know. So now I talk about RAM and hard discs, my mouse and Norton Utilities.

Humans continue to grow and mature till the day they die. We are gaining new knowledge and skills every day and we need to eat good, solid food to keep our bodies working efficiently. If I went back to drinking only milk I'm sure I would soon find myself sick and unable to do all the things I enjoy.

So now it is time to grow. The Bible contains the spiritual food you need in order to grow spiritually. We read Paul's words: 'All Scripture is given by inspiration of God, and is profitable for doctrine, for reproof, for correction, for instruction in righteousness, that the man of God may be complete, thoroughly equipped for every good work' (2 Timothy 3:16-17). Open your Bible and start reading and meditating upon those hard-to-understand parts so that you might grow in your faith.

Just like the house that is being built, I trust and pray that you will become a mature Christian, and so be of great use in Christ's kingdom. May God bless you with spiritual growth as you go through these chapters.

To think about

1. What is meant by repentance?
2. Did Christ have to repent? Explain the reasons for your answer.
3. How do Christians grow spiritually?
4. Parents, what are you doing to help your children grow in their knowledge of Christ?
5. Children, what are you doing to increase your knowledge of the teachings of God as they are found in the Bible?

Covered in mud

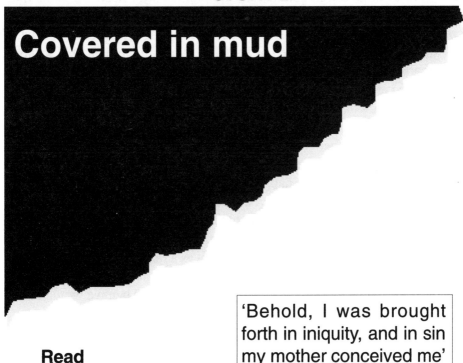

Read
• • • • • • • • • • • • • • • • • • •
Romans 3:9-20

> 'Behold, I was brought forth in iniquity, and in sin my mother conceived me' (Psalm 51:5).

In this chapter we are beginning a short series which has something to do with the word 'TULIP'. I'm sure some parents reading this book will have seen this term used in other Christian books and will know that each letter of the word stands for a great truth taught in the Scriptures. We shall look at one of these letters in each of chapters 2-6.

The letter T stands for 'Total depravity', and I'm sure most of my young readers will say, 'Whatever does this mean? It's too hard for me to understand!'

I'd like to explain what these words mean. They are saying that we are all guilty of sin, which is breaking God's law, or not doing what God has commanded.

Today most people don't like talking about sin. In many churches even pastors don't like telling the members of their congregation they are sinners who need Christ as their Saviour. But sin is our problem and, whether we like it or not, the day will come when each one of us will stand before the judgement seat of Christ. If our sins have not been forgiven by the Lord Jesus, Judgement Day will be a day of absolute terror for us.

If you have read any of my other Family Reading books you will already know that I grew up on a farm and that I have one brother, John. John and I have always got on very well together and even now we still think it is great to visit each other. We are both Christians, both were schoolteachers many years ago, and we both became pastors. Often we sit and talk, laughing about funny events that happened when we were young.

We loved swimming in the river. We spent many hours climbing a huge tree with branches reaching out over the water. Not only did we climb the tree, but we crawled carefully out along the branches till we were over the deep water — and then we would jump. It was a real thrill falling down and splashing into the water. It wasn't long before we made ourselves a swing. We tied one end of the rope to the end of the branch. Then we would swing out from the bank, letting go when we were well out over the water.

On the hot afternoons after school we spent many enjoyable hours on the riverbank, swimming and eating water melons.

There were also times when we had our friends come to visit us and together we all had a great time. Sometimes we played pranks on each other.

I would like to tell you about one of these occasions. The rest of us decided that we would throw handfuls of mud at John as he came out of the river. Poor John! As he started to climb up the riverbank, mud started flying in his direction. The first time he laughed and dived back into the river to clean himself up.

As he began to climb out a second time, he was once more pelted with mud. Again he laughed and dived back into the river.

However, the third time when he was splattered with mud the smile disappeared. He accidentally slipped down the riverbank and fell into the mud at the river's edge. When he pulled himself back up the bank more mud splashed over him. He was covered in mud from head to foot. There was mud in his hair, in his ears, in his eyes — over every part of his body. John tried to wipe some of the mud off but regardless of what he did the mud was still there. When we tried to help him clean up we found that the mud got on us and made us dirty too.

To get John clean we took him home and hosed him down. Finally, he stood there as clean as he had ever been.

The state of John when he was all covered in mud is a picture of human beings covered in sin. Every person born into this world, with the exception of Christ (and Adam and Eve at the time of their creation) has a sinful nature. In the Garden of Eden our representative Adam sinned — he broke the law of God. His sin became our sin and sin has infected every part of our nature. Just as John was totally covered with mud, so also we are born totally infected with sin. Actually, sin is even worse than the mud that only covered John's skin on the outside. It is rather like a bad case of measles. Not only is the rash seen on the skin, but the disease also infects our inner being. In the same way, sin has infected our bodies, hearts, minds, emotions — in fact every part of us. This is what we mean when we speak of people being 'totally depraved'. It doesn't mean that we are as bad as we could be. Humans still know that God exists. Each person has a conscience which should be used as our guide in many aspects of life. However, even the conscience has been stained by sin and needs training.

'Total depravity' means that sin has hurt us so much that we cannot reach out to find God. We are spiritually dead. Our reading describes what we are like:

There is none righteous, no, not one...
There is none who seeks after God...
There is no fear of God before their eyes

(Romans 3:10,11,18).

Spiritually we are like Lazarus who had died and was completely powerless to help himself (Ephesians 2:1). He needed the Lord Jesus to raise him from the dead (see John 11:43).

In order for any of us to be saved God must act. He must send the Holy Spirit into our hearts and give us spiritual life. We must be set free from sin (Romans 6:18). When this happens we are able to love and serve Jesus Christ as our Lord and Saviour.

What we all need to understand is that we sin because we are sinners. When the Holy Spirit makes us aware of our sins we shall then understand that we need a Saviour to cleanse us from our sin and unrighteousness.

May all my readers know for themselves the blessing of eternal life in Jesus Christ.

To think about

1. What is sin? Make a list of sins commonly found in society today.
2. Where do we find the law of God?
3. What does the word 'total' mean in the expression 'total depravity'?
4. How is it possible to get rid of the stain of sin?
5. This story shows the effects of sin — how unkind we were to John! We should not treat our brother, sister, or friend as my friends and I treated John that day.

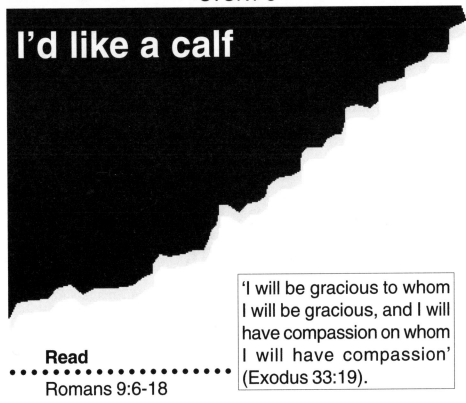

I'd like a calf

Read
• • • • • • • • • • • • • • • • • • • •
Romans 9:6-18

'I will be gracious to whom I will be gracious, and I will have compassion on whom I will have compassion' (Exodus 33:19).

We come in this chapter to the letter U in TULIP, which stands for 'Unconditional Election'. In the previous chapter we saw that babies are born into the world with a sinful nature. Sad to say, we are all sinners and without God's love and grace no one would be saved. God could simply have decided to leave us to suffer what we deserve.

However, God planned to save many sinners from all ages and all parts of the world. He set his love upon a people and this meant that he chose to save certain individuals even though they had nothing lovable about them. God has every right to make such decisions because he is the Lord of all things and he alone has the right to do as he pleases with rebellious people.

God hates sin, yet he showed his great love by sending Christ into the world to save those people whom he had chosen for salvation.

In the Old Testament days God set his love upon Abraham. Of all the people in the world at that time, Abraham became the 'friend of God'. God chose him to be the father of a special people — the Israelites. There was nothing special about Abraham before God chose him and called him. He was a pagan who had no interest in the living God. However, God decided that it would be Abraham whom he would make his friend.

In Deuteronomy 7:6-8 we read God's words to the Israelites: 'For you are a holy people to the LORD your God; the LORD your God has chosen you to be a people for himself, a special treasure above all the peoples on the face of the earth. The LORD did not set his love on you nor choose you because you were more in number than any other people, for you were the least of all peoples; but because the LORD loves you…' God chose Israel to be his and the reason for his choice can only be found in his mind.

When John and I were schoolboys we had many jobs to do on the farm. It wasn't hard work, even though we complained that we had no time to play. We collected the eggs, helped with the milking, made sure Mum had wood for the kitchen stove and at times we minded the cows. One job we particularly enjoyed was feeding the calves. We spent many happy hours with them.

One day we decided to ask Dad to give each of us a calf we could call our own. Pointing to the calves we wanted we promised that we would take good care of them. We both picked calves that looked healthy and had a happy nature.

Dad listened carefully to John and me and then said that he had already decided to give us each a calf. Yes, we had to make promises to look after the calves we received. Then Dad announced which calf would belong to John and which one would be mine.

'But that's not the one I wanted,' I complained. However, Dad had made his choice and there was nothing I could do about it except say, 'Thanks, Dad.'

During the months that followed I grew to love that calf. I fed it twice each day, played with it and made sure it was well groomed. But

why Dad gave me that particular calf I never found out. He made the choice for some reason he alone knew.

So also when God chose a people for salvation he made the choice for reasons known only to himself. The apostle Paul simply says, 'He chose us in him [Christ] before the foundation of the world' (Ephesians 1:4). This is an amazing truth: God chose a people to be saved before the world was created and he gave them to his Son, the Lord Jesus Christ.

In our reading, the two boys Jacob and Esau are mentioned. God chose Jacob as the one he loved. Why Jacob? The answer is, 'I don't know.' However, God knows why he made such a choice. Jacob was an annoying boy who cheated his brother and tricked his father. However, God worked in his life so that in time he became a man of true faith and the father of a great nation, Israel.

As we look around us we find that not many people are Christians. However, God does have a people who love him and there are two passages of Scripture that give us a clue to the reasons for God's choice of a person to be saved.

First, Paul says, 'Not many wise…, not many mighty, not many noble, are called. But God has chosen the foolish things of the world to put to shame the wise, and God has chosen the weak things of the world to put to shame the things which are mighty … that no flesh should glory in his presence' (1 Corinthians 1:26-29).

Secondly, James writes, 'Has God not chosen the poor of this world to be rich in faith and heirs of the kingdom which he promised to those who love him?' (James 2:5).

I'm sure if you or I were making the choice of a people to inherit a kingdom we would pick out the nicest people — the kind people, good-looking people, people who would love us. Yes, I'm sure we would pick the 'good' people. However, the reason for God's particular choice is found in God alone — there are no 'conditions' that God foresaw in men which caused him to love them.

The doctrine of unconditional election can seem most unfair to most people. But we must remember that God did not have to save anybody or everybody. The Bible tells us that it is not just a few people who are saved, but rather a great number of people from all ages and all the nations of the earth — 'a great multitude which no one could number' (Revelation 7:9). If you have the time, read Luke 14:15-24 and there you will learn that God's kingdom will be completely filled by a large number of people who have repented of their sins. God is a very generous, loving God.

There are many people who say, 'What's the use of following Christ? I might not be one of God's chosen people. It doesn't matter what I do. If God hasn't chosen me to be saved I can't do anything about it.' We must not think that way. God has not revealed a list of his chosen — 'elect' — people, but he has revealed a great truth: 'Believe on the Lord Jesus Christ, and you will be saved' (Acts 16:31). This is what matters as far as you and I are concerned. God has promised that all who trust in Jesus Christ for salvation will be saved. If you trust your salvation to Christ he will never fail you.

To think about

1. What relationship was Jacob to Esau and who was the elder?
2. What does it mean when you read, 'Believe on the Lord Jesus Christ'?
3. God chose Abraham to be his friend. Why?
4. What is the purpose of election?
5. Why should God choose you for salvation?

Special care

'The Son of Man did not come to be served, but to serve, and to give his life a ransom for many' (Matthew 20:28).

We now come to the letter L in TULIP. This stands for 'Limited Atonement' and means that the Lord Jesus Christ came into the world to save those people who were given to him by his Father. Jesus did not come into the world to make the salvation of all people possible, but to make certain the salvation of his chosen people.

God chose a people to be saved, and in time Jesus Christ came into the world to be their substitute. He lived a life of total obedience to God and died upon a cross, bearing their punishment. Jesus Christ was the sin-bearer on behalf of his people. He lived and died for those who were to be saved — and for them alone.

This does not mean that only God's people benefit from Christ's life and death. The Bible reminds us that God 'makes his sun rise on the evil and on the good, and sends rain on the just and on the unjust' (Matthew 5:45). As God blesses his people some of the blessings also benefit others. But the blessing of salvation belongs to those alone who are the gift of the Father to his Son.

In the last chapter I told you about Dad giving my brother and me each a calf to call our own. When we found out which were our calves we went

down to the paddock and caught them. We started to spend a lot of time with our special calves. I would brush mine down and always make sure it had a little more to drink and eat than all the other calves. When we played with the animals, it was our calves that received the special attention. John and I knew that our calves were special. They belonged to us! We gave them each a name and when we called them they trotted over to us for a pat on the head. The other calves took little notice of us except when it was feeding-time. Then they came over to get their share. So every calf in the paddock benefited from the special attention we gave to the ones we owned.

Then came the day when Dad decided he would sell some of the cattle. Both John and I were worried that our calves might be sent to the auction sale, but that didn't happen. They belonged to us. The others were sold and some ended up on new farms where they were cared for by their new owners. Others I think ended up at the abattoirs.

Our two calves eventually grew up and became part of the milking herd. Even as fully grown cows they still came to us when we called them, stretching out their heads for a pat and a rub. We loved our special pet calves. In time they had calves of their own. Eventually too John and I grew up and left home, and I don't know what happened to those cows which once were our pets.

The special treatment we gave those calves reminds me of the way Christ deals with those whom the Father gave to him. He loves us and saved us from God's punishment

which was due to us because of our sins. For his people he built the 'salvation bridge' from heaven to earth. He did everything that was necessary for his people to be saved.

When all is quiet and you are alone think of the saving love of the Lord Jesus Christ for his people. Christ said, 'Greater love has no one than this, than to lay down one's life for his friends' (John 15:13). This our Saviour did for his people. Paul, when writing to the church at Ephesus, spoke of Christ's love for his church. He said, 'Christ also loved the church and gave himself for her' (Ephesians 5:25).

It is wonderful to have God as your heavenly Father. How sad it is that there are so many people who love their sins and are members of Satan's family! Jesus spoke very plainly to some of the Jews who were arguing with him: 'You are of your father the devil' (John 8:44).

You might ask the question: 'How do I know if Jesus Christ died for me? How do I know if I am one of Christ's people?' The answer is simple. Have you repented of your sins and are you trusting in the Lord Jesus Christ for your salvation? If so, then you are one of those chosen by God for salvation — you are one of that great number for whom Christ lived and died.

Christ invites sinners to come to him and be saved. His invitation is made sincerely. If you come you will be saved. I pray that you will be able to say with the apostle Paul, 'I live by faith in the Son of God, who loved me and gave himself for me' (Galatians 2:20).

To think about

1. What is meant by 'limited atonement'?
2. What is the future of all those for whom Christ died?
3. What blessings did Christ win for his people both in this life and the life to come?

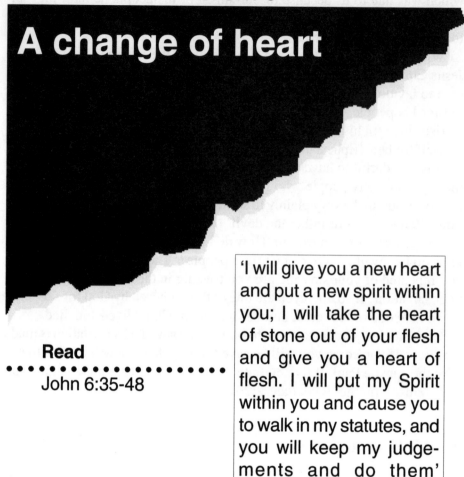

A change of heart

Read

John 6:35-48

> 'I will give you a new heart and put a new spirit within you; I will take the heart of stone out of your flesh and give you a heart of flesh. I will put my Spirit within you and cause you to walk in my statutes, and you will keep my judgements and do them' (Ezekiel 36:26-27).

We now come to the letter I in the word 'TULIP'. It stands for 'Irresistible Grace'. What do we mean by this expression?

So far we have seen the work of both the Father and the Son in the salvation of sinners. The Father chose a people to give to his Son. In turn the Son agreed to come into the world and live and die as their substitute. However, that was not all. The saving work of Christ must be applied to the hearts of each of his people. Now we come to the work of the Holy Spirit, because he must take Christ's salvation and apply it to his chosen people.

We have all heard of very sick people who are in need of a heart transplant. Some time ago I read of a young girl who was desperately ill. Her

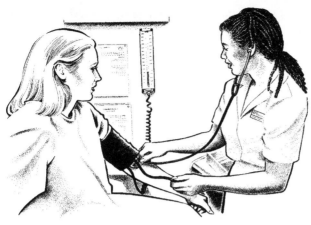

heart muscle was not working and she was expected to die soon. At school she had been very good at sports, a girl who enjoyed living a very energetic life, but now there was little she could do except lie very still in her hospital bed.

Then it was reported on the TV that a new heart had become available and the surgery to give her a heart transplant had been carried out successfully. When we heard the news we thanked God for the skill given to the surgeons. Some time later we read that the girl was back at school, studying hard and once again playing the sports she loved but had previously not been able to take part in. Life had changed dramatically for this young lady — not because of anything she had done, but because of the gift of a new heart and the skill of the doctors who cared for her. She was a new person and said that a new life had started for her. So it is when a person is born again.

Sinners have no real interest in the living God. Paul wrote, 'There is none who seeks after God' (Romans 3:11). When the good news of Christ's salvation is preached people don't all jump to their feet and run to Christ to be saved. Without the work of the Holy Spirit in their hearts they will all go home and forget what they heard.

Our text tells us that God will remove the cold heart of stone and replace it with a heart of flesh, a heart that loves the Lord Jesus Christ. This, of course, is not a heart transplant that is carried out by doctors. The Holy Spirit transforms God's chosen people into new people. Paul wrote to the Ephesian believers, 'We are his workmanship, created in Christ Jesus for good works...' (Ephesians 2:10). Jesus Christ told Nicodemus that the work of the new birth was the work of the Holy Spirit (John 3:3-8).

Now God doesn't force sinners into his kingdom while they shout out that they don't want to be members of it. The Holy Spirit brings about the new birth in

the sinner's heart. When that person hears the gospel he or she will willingly turn to Christ for salvation. By the power of the Holy Spirit the person responds to the gospel call.

The Holy Spirit makes it possible for sinners to repent of their sins. In addition the Holy Spirit gives to every sinner who repents the faith that is necessary to unite him or her to Christ. All the blessings that Christ won for his people come through this God-given faith.

We know why one person who hears the gospel goes to Christ in repentance, yet a hundred others who hear the same gospel message go home unaffected. It is because that one person has been born again — 'born, not of blood, nor of the will of the flesh, nor of the will of man, but of God' (John 1:13). All who are born of the Holy Spirit hate their sins and want to live in a way which is pleasing to God.

The Holy Spirit often uses the preaching of the Word to call people to faith in Christ. Other people may be convicted of their sins as they read the Bible or some book which explains the teachings of Scripture. Sometimes something happens in a person's life that causes him or her to turn to Christ. It could be the death of a friend or relative, or the loss of something of great value. Some have been brought to faith in Christ because the Holy Spirit caused them to wonder what life was all about. Without God, life is senseless. The Holy Spirit works in many intriguing ways to bring sinners to faith in the Saviour.

So it is that Christ, through his Spirit, gives eternal life to all who were given to him by his Father. God draws his people to Christ and on the last day he will change their mortal bodies into wonderful, incorruptible bodies like the resurrected body of the Lord Jesus Christ.

Irresistible grace, then, is God's goodness in changing a sinner's heart, mind and will so that he or she willingly turns to Christ for salvation. The salvation of any person does not depend upon that person's intelligence or supposed goodness — it is totally dependent upon the grace of God. This means that the Christian will give God all the glory for his or her salvation. We contributed nothing towards our salvation; God did it all.

To think about

1. What can a sinner do to cause the Holy Spirit to give him or her a new heart?
2. Who are the people given a new heart by the Holy Spirit?
3. What is meant by the word 'grace'?
4. You may spend hours witnessing to others of Christ's salvation and yet they do not repent and turn to him. Why is that so? What can you do to bring the sinner to repentance?

Safe and secure

Read
Romans 8:29-39

> 'My sheep hear my voice, and I know them, and they follow me. And I give them eternal life, and they shall never perish; neither shall anyone snatch them out of my hand. My Father, who has given them to me, is greater than all; and no one is able to snatch them out of my Father's hand' (John 10:27-29).

We now come to the final letter in the word 'TULIP'. The 'P' stands for 'Perseverance of the Saints'. This simply means that those who were chosen by God for salvation and given to the Lord Jesus Christ will persevere in their Christian lives until that day when they are in heaven with the Lord. Faithfulness is impossible without the help of God and we only persevere because God perseveres with us.

All who are born again are united for ever to the Lord Jesus Christ and, as our reading says, nothing 'shall be able to separate us from the love of God which is in Christ Jesus our Lord' (Romans 8:39). True believers will often fall into sin, but they will never return permanently to those sinful ways. They are new creations and the power of sin does not rule their lives.

God will bring them to repentance because he is all-powerful. We should rejoice when we read these words of Jude:

Now to him who is able to keep you from stumbling,
And to present you faultless
Before the presence of his glory with exceeding joy…

(Jude 24).

Australia is well known for sailing races which attract entrants from all parts of the world. Recently in one of those races two events took place which illustrate the truth of today's subject.

While the race was in progress one boat had a very serious accident. During the night a sailor fell overboard. This meant that the boat had to turn round and begin the search for the missing sailor. The sea was very rough with plenty of waves breaking over the boat. Even with strong torches lighting up the area, the sailor could not be found. It was not till several days later that his body was recovered.

On another boat the same thing happened during the night. A sailor fell overboard, but this time precautions had been taken to ensure his safety. A rope had been attached to his harness at one end and to the boat at the other. When his friends heard him call as he fell, they ran to the rope and pulled him back onto the boat. He had a few bruises from bumping against the ship's side, but he was safe and secure and able to get on with his work. We should note that his security and rescue did not depend upon the sailor himself, but upon the wisdom of the people who had installed the safety precautions on the boat, and on the other sailors, who pulled him back on board.

Eternal life is the possession of God's people from the moment they believe, and from that time onwards they are kept secure by God's almighty power. Christians persevere because God perseveres with them. One writer put it like this: 'I hold and am being held.'

We all admire people who keep on trying till they achieve their goal. One day I sat down and watched a small ant trying to drag a little piece of food along a track. It was obvious it was trying to get the food back to the ants' nest. It must have been hard work, but the ant didn't give up. After a while another ant came scurrying along and together they set to work dragging the piece of food home. Soon yet another ant arrived on the scene and it wasn't long before I saw the piece of food disappearing along the ant track under the overhanging grass. The ants persevered and I guess they achieved their goal.

So it must be with each one of Christ's people. Having begun the Christian life, we must remain faithful till life's end. Yes, we shall fall into sin many times, but God will lift us up again and bring us to repentance. He will make sure that each one of his people reaches heaven safely.

And how can you be assured that you belong to Christ? When you see that you are living a holy life because you love God and are looking forward with joyful anticipation to the time when you will be with your Saviour! One of the greatest proofs that you belong to Christ is that you are faithful to him day after day! May God be pleased to bless you as you serve the Lord Jesus. Rejoice in your salvation and show that you love God by obeying his commands, as found in Scripture.

To think about

1. What does each of the letters in the word TULIP stand for?
2. Explain what is meant by the words of John 3:16.
3. Why is it possible for God to keep his people faithful throughout their Christian lives?

Practise what you preach

Read
. . . .
1 Corinthians 9:24-27

Recently Val and I received a gift of two tickets to see an Irish dance group, called Riverdance, which was touring the world. I'm not a dance fan, but was amazed at the precision of this dance group. They all clicked their heels at the same time, the tapping sound was synchronized perfectly and the jumps and twirls were all in perfect unison. While driving home after the show we talked about the amount of time they must have spent practising.

Many people sacrifice a tremendous amount of time learning skills to use in the sports they love. Others practise for thousands of hours to learn the skills they need to play the piano or other musical instruments. It all takes time and energy.

I spend a lot of time in front of my computer typing. Val, the children and now the grandchildren tell me I should learn to type. 'If you learn to type you will be twice as fast and be able to write so much more,' they keep saying. So I purchased a typing programme and started. It meant I had to learn the position of the keys on the keyboard. It was all hopeless. I couldn't type as quickly as I could with my two fingers and instead of producing accurate type it came out something like 'I fo honr racj aftwfnoom.' I just gave up and went back to my two faithful fingers.

However, I admire all those who stick at something till they achieve their goal. The athletes who win medals at the Olympic Games are usually people who have trained for years — and all for the glory of competing and if possible winning a medal. In the ancient Olympic Games, about which the apostle Paul spoke, there were rules for all who competed. They had to swear an oath that they had spent a certain length of time training according to the rules and regulations. They kept to a strict diet and trained every day in the hope that they would win a laurel wreath. If they won that precious prize I doubt whether they would have still had it in one piece by the time they returned home. It would  no doubt have fallen apart. Today the medal winners take great care of their prizes, but even so I wonder where the medals will be in a thousand years?

The apostle Paul compared the Christian life to a race, saying it was a very serious business. He wrote that he worked hard to control his body because he knew that it often caused him to sin. Paul was not saying that his body was evil in itself, but he knew that he sinned using his eyes, ears and mouth etc. We all know that there are times when our eyes see something and then we want, or covet, that object for ourselves. We hear words that are shameful and so often we ourselves say words which are hurtful. Our bodies can become lazy and there are times when we overeat. As a result of things we have seen and heard we think thoughts of which we should be ashamed. And of course all too often we use our hands and feet to do things we should not do, or to go to places where we should not be.

With so many temptations to sin involving our bodies there is a real need for us to keep them under control and this requires effort. 'I discipline my body,' said Paul and if we belong to Christ we must do the same.

I have to discipline my body by controlling what my eyes see. This means I only watch on TV programmes that are good, wholesome and instructive, and I don't go to those places that cause me to see and think sinful thoughts. I make a real effort to control my tongue. I make sure I don't swear and I don't tell dirty stories. I enjoy food, so I have to be careful to avoid being a glutton. It is easy to become lazy, so I make sure I don't spend too much of my time resting when I should be doing something useful.

Then there are the positive things I must do. I have to make time for prayer and Bible reading. I tell my body to get out of bed and go to the worship service or the prayer meeting instead of being idle.

Our bodies must be used in the service of God instead of Satan. This requires effort and, praise God, we can have the victory. If we are born again we are in the Christian race. The power of sin in our lives has been broken and with God's help we are now able to live godly lives which glorify our Saviour, the Lord Jesus Christ.

The prize is eternal life in the presence of the Lord Jesus Christ, and all who complete the race will receive that honour. Some Christians will receive a great reward on Judgement Day while others will receive smaller rewards, but all who complete the course will receive the 'crown of life'.

If you have just commenced the Christian race you will need to make a real effort to control your body. Others may be getting very close to the finishing line. They too must control their bodies.

The apostle Paul concluded this section of Scripture by saying that he was setting an example of Christian living for all to follow. He disciplined his body to make sure he finished the race. What a terrible situation it would have been if Paul had not 'practised what he preached'! He would have been guilty of hypocrisy. No, Paul knew that people did not sleep their way into heaven. Effort is required, and part of that effort is controlling the body.

Some people try to force themselves to live a life of obedience to the commands of Christ by their own efforts. These people are no better than the Pharisees who thought they could win God's approval by obedience. All who are born of the Holy Spirit find that their lives are controlled by the Spirit. It is 'by the Spirit' that God's people are able to put to death their sinful ways. By ourselves we shall never have the victory over sin. The apostle Paul put it this way: 'Therefore, my beloved, as you have always obeyed ... work out your own salvation with fear and trembling; for it is God who works in you both to will and to do for his good pleasure' (Philippians 2:12-13).

There are others who have not even reached the starting-line. If you are one of those people, go to the Lord Jesus and ask him to forgive your sins and make you a new person. Then he will send the Holy Spirit into your heart and you too will be able to take part in the Christian race.

To think about

1. What is the 'imperishable crown' that Christians receive at the end of life? (See 1 Corinthians 9:25; James 1:12).
2. Paul disciplined his body. Make a list of ways Christians should discipline their bodies.
3. How do you join the Christian race?
4. What will be the result if people do not join the Christian race?

Forgiven and forgotten

Read
● ● ● ● ● ● ● ● ● ● ● ● ● ● ● ● ● ● ●
Jeremiah 31:31-40

'For I will forgive their iniquity, and their sin I will remember no more' (Jeremiah 31:34).

How quickly we forget! Then suddenly everything flashes back into the memory. Just recently I returned to my old congregation to introduce a visiting preacher to the members. I was overjoyed that they asked me to visit them for a couple of weeks. Their visitor came from Scotland and was to spend three Lord's Days with them. I was to have the privilege of looking after Sam and making him known to everyone. However, I was soon to discover how quickly I had forgotten many things about a place which had been my home for over eight years.

First, I discovered that the town had grown and I became lost when driving to an outlying church. I had to stop the car and ask a man walking a dog if he could show me the way. Sam found it hard to believe that I was so forgetful.

When travelling between churches I became

confused. There were new roads leading off the route that I once knew so well. I suddenly discovered I wasn't sure which way to go. On one occasion I drove three times round a roundabout before I remembered which exit I was to take.

Then came the time for me to introduce Sam to the people who made up the congregation. I found that at times I became flustered and, looking at a sea of faces, I discovered that I couldn't quickly remember the names of people I had known so well.

I'm sure that many people reading these words have experienced the same kind of thing. I felt embarrassed and laughed saying that I must be getting old and that my brain was not working as well as in my younger days. Maybe that was the truth!

We can all be very forgetful when we should remember things. Young people forget their homework. Many forget to do the jobs Mum and Dad have asked them to do each week. Mums and dads forget they have to take children to sporting events. We all forget at times!

Sometimes, especially during the quiet of night before I fall asleep, I remember things I couldn't remember during the day. Then there are times when I remember events that happened many years before — some of them events that I wish I could forget for ever. I remember sins I committed years ago and had forgotten. This upsets me greatly as I am a Christian and hate sin. My sins, which had been forgotten and out of my mind, are remembered once again. I'm sure many of my readers have also had this experience. When this happens I once again pray to God asking that I might be forgiven for the sake of the Lord Jesus Christ.

We have a wonderful God who loves his Son, the Lord Jesus Christ. That love is also for all those whom he has given to his Son and for whom the Lord Jesus died. Jesus came into this world for one great purpose — to glorify God in the salvation of sinners. By his life and death Jesus saved his people. He died that we might be forgiven, and throughout the Scriptures we read that our sins are forgiven if we confess them to God in true repentance. The apostle John wrote, 'If we confess our sins, he is faithful and just to forgive us our sins and to cleanse us from all unrighteousness' (1 John 1:9). This is a wonderful truth. In his own death Jesus Christ washed our sins away! He died so that his people might live.

There are many people today who consider the death of the Lord Jesus to be the death of a martyr — the death of a great man who died for what he believed. Let us always remember that Jesus Christ was the Son of God who died upon the cross as the 'sin-bearer', bearing the sins of his people. He died, being punished by God, in the place of his people.

Now the sins of his people are forgiven when they repent, as our text tells us — they will be forgiven and remembered no more. This is what I want — that my sins should be forgotten and remembered no more. I thank God that the day is coming when I will stand before the judgement throne of Christ my Saviour to hear his words: 'Forgiven! Forgotten!' I know this truth now, but I long to hear it from the lips of Christ and know that I will never again be plagued by the thoughts of my sins. God will have forgotten, and so will I. On that day all of Christ's redeemed people will look upon the face of their precious Saviour and praise him and give him thanks for ever and ever.

Again on that day all God's people will know the truth of the words written by Micah:

Who is a God like you,
Pardoning iniquity
And passing over the transgression of the remnant of his heritage?
He does not retain his anger for ever,
Because he delights in mercy…
You will cast all our sins
Into the depths of the sea

(Micah 7: 18-19).

May we all be able to praise God for his saving goodness!

To think about

1. Why does God find sin to be so horrid?
2. Why should God forget and forgive your sins?
3. God is 'holy'. What does that mean?

An unforgettable wedding

Read
• • • • • • • • • • • • • • • • • • • •
Matthew 22:1-14

'Let us be glad and rejoice and give him glory, for the marriage of the Lamb has come, and his wife has made herself ready' (Revelation 19:7).

I'm sure all married people can remember something about the day they were married. It is, after all, rather an important day. On the day of my marriage a criminal had escaped from the local prison and almost every person travelling to the wedding was stopped and in some cases was asked to open the car boot so the police could make sure no one was hiding there. When the car in which I was travelling was pulled over by the police, the officer just laughed and waved us on.

Today my friend Sam had a phone call from his wife in Scotland and he came to me afterwards laughing — although I'm sure the event wasn't very funny at all for the people involved.

Today is quite a hot day in our part of Australia and it is difficult to believe that

in Scotland the snow is falling. In fact the snow is several feet deep around Sam's manse near Loch Ness. I think the bride must have been disappointed with the weather. It was cold and damp. However, it was her wedding day and she duly arrived at the church for this most important ceremony to take place. People had gathered outside the church building to catch a glimpse of the beautiful bride with her attendants at her side. But just as she was about to enter the church she slipped on a snow-covered step and fell. A gasp went up as she quickly struggled to her feet. She was all right, but there on her lovely white gown was a dirty mark. It was obvious that she was upset.

Soon the wedding was underway, but the snow started falling as a fierce gale started to blow. By the time the wedding guests moved to the hall for the reception several feet of snow surrounded the building. A few people looked at their parked cars and shook their heads.

The wind blew, the snow kept on falling, and when the time arrived for the newly married couple to leave the hall for their honeymoon they could hardly open the door. When they eventually did they discovered to their horror that the parked cars could not be seen. Everything was hidden under a heavy blanket of pure white snow. The bride and groom were trapped in the church hall with all the guests.

A quick phone call revealed that more snow was on the way and everyone was forced to spend the night in the church hall. That married couple would always remember their wedding — they had a story to tell their children and grandchildren.

The Bible speaks of a heavenly wedding feast which is a symbolical way of describing the time when we shall enjoy the presence of Christ for ever. This looks forward to that great day when the church (the bride) will sit down with her husband, the Lord Jesus Christ, to celebrate their wedding, their union for all eternity. The church will be dressed in the perfect righteousness of the Lord Jesus and the acts of obedience to Christ done in his name. This church will have been made perfect by her husband and Saviour. Only those who are born again, and so united to Christ, will have a seat at that wedding feast.

Today's reading describes a wedding that took place a long time ago. The custom of that day was for all who attended to be given a special cloak to wear as they entered the wedding reception. Christ's parable speaks of a man who sneaked into a royal wedding dressed in only his own clothing. The king, who was the host, had the man thrown out. He called his servants and said, 'Bind him hand and foot, take him away, and cast him into outer darkness; there will be weeping and gnashing of teeth.' What a horrible situation for that man! He should have been dressed in the special wedding clothes which were freely available from the king.

The day is coming when our Saviour, Jesus Christ, will return to this world in power and glory to gather his people together for that great wedding feast. Each one of his people will be clothed in the God-given righteousness of Christ. They will be glorious to behold because not only are they Christ's people, but they will then have their resurrection bodies, similar to that of their Saviour. Each one will have been made perfect in righteousness.

Christ's people will come from all parts of the world and from all periods of history. All will be united to Christ by the great work of God's Holy Spirit. All will be forgiven and perfect in every way. Together they will all rejoice at that great wedding. Their hearts will be filled with love for God and their Saviour, their heavenly Bridegroom, the Lord Jesus.

Together they will praise God with the words of Scripture: 'Alleluia! For the Lord God Omnipotent reigns! Let us be glad and rejoice and give him glory, for the marriage of the Lamb has come, and his wife has made herself ready' (Revelation 19:6-7). They will enjoy for ever the home he has prepared for them.

It is my hope and prayer that all who read these words may have wedding garments prepared for them, on which their names are clearly written for all to see.

To think about

1. Who is the Lamb of God, and why does he have that title?
2. What is meant by 'the resurrection body' and how does it differ from the body we each now have? (Read 1 Corinthians 15:35-49).
3. Why do we need to be holy in order to enter heaven?

The best spectacles of all

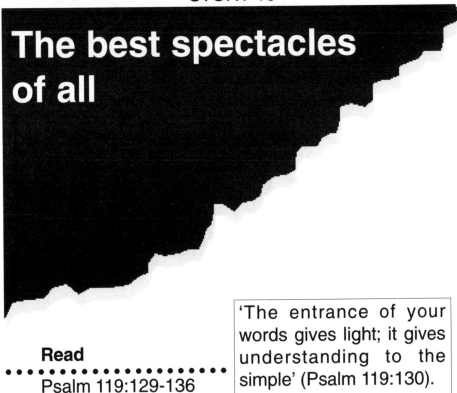

Read
• • • • • • • • • • • • • • • • • •
Psalm 119:129-136

'The entrance of your words gives light; it gives understanding to the simple' (Psalm 119:130).

Recently my eyesight deteriorated and I found difficulty in seeing small things. I discovered that my arms were not long enough to hold a book far away from my eyes in order to read it. Consequently my daughter Heather, who is an optician, decided it was time to check my eyes and soon I was wearing a new pair of spectacles. I could see well again and no longer needed long arms in order to read my books. A pair of glasses is vital for people who have poor eyesight.

Some time ago I wanted to examine the moon and a friend lent me a telescope for a couple of nights. I saw things on the surface of the moon I had never seen before. On another occasion I used a microscope to look at very small insects. I could see them all very clearly. Glasses of various kinds are most useful in our daily life.

As I was talking to a friend about my new glasses he said, 'Do you know what is the best pair of spectacles in the world?'

I thought for a while. I had once tried bifocals and trifocals and found them useless. Now I was using varifocals, or multifocals as we call them, and suggested they were the best of all.

However my friend said, 'The best spectacles of all are your Bible.'

'How can that be?' I asked.

'Well,' he said, 'If you want to see yourself as God sees you, look in the Bible. The Bible will show you what you are like — a sinner who needs a Saviour.'

Then he went on to say, 'If you want to know more about God, then read your Bible, for it is like a pair of glasses. It will reveal to you what God is like. It will tell you that God is spirit and that he is perfectly holy in all his ways. He hates sin and will punish all who die without having repented of their sins. Yes, the Bible is a good pair of spectacles by which we see ourselves as we really are — sinners in need of a Saviour.'

'Is that all?' I asked.

'There's more,' he replied. 'If you want to know about things that happened a long time ago, or things that are yet to happen in the future, your Bible is like a telescope. It reveals all you need to know about creation — that God created the heavens and the earth, the angels and Adam and Eve. It also reveals what will happen in the future. The most wonderful event will be the return of the Lord Jesus Christ. Yes, the Bible is like a telescope!'

'And is that all?' I again asked.

'No,' he replied, 'there is still more. The Bible is like a microscope. The Bible exposes the innermost secrets of our heart. It convicts us of sins we did not know we were committing. It makes us look at the motives for all that we do. Others cannot see into our hearts, but with the guidance of God's Word we can see into our own hearts.'

So each one of us must read the Bible, acknowledging that it is the searching and revealing Word of God. It is God's word to sinners calling them to repentance and faith in Christ. And it is the encouraging Word of God which contains the wonderful promises made to all who love the Lord Jesus Christ.

The Bible is a spiritual pair of glasses that everyone should have. So take out your Bible and if there is dust on the cover blow it off and read, praying that God might show you your need of a Saviour. Pray that God might show you how much he loves his people and lead you to know Christ as your Lord and Saviour.

To think about

1. What are bifocals?
2. The Bible contains words and sentences which we can easily read for ourselves, yet most people do not understand the great truths that are taught on its pages. Why is this? Read 1 Corinthians 2:10-14.
3. How do you feel about the fact that God can look into your heart and mind? What can we do so that we can say Psalm 139:23 with a clear conscience? (Read Jeremiah 17:9-10).

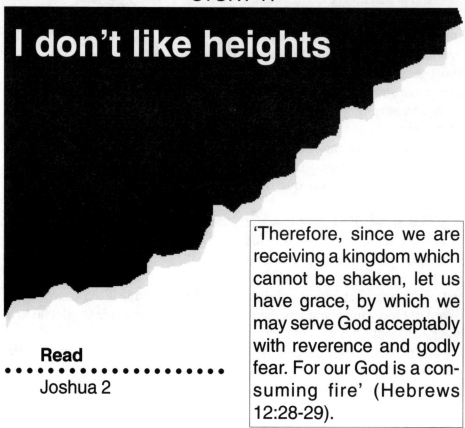

I don't like heights

Read
• • • • • • • • • • • • • • • • • • • •
Joshua 2

'Therefore, since we are receiving a kingdom which cannot be shaken, let us have grace, by which we may serve God acceptably with reverence and godly fear. For our God is a consuming fire' (Hebrews 12:28-29).

Today many Christians seem to have no holy 'fear' of God. People come to the place of worship unprepared in many ways — sloppily dressed, laughing and talking about worldly things. When they are seated very few, if any, bow their heads in prayer, seeking the blessing of God upon their time of worship. Too many professing Christians have no real hatred of sin and live for themselves and the things of the world. They believe that all is well with their souls because they spend an hour or so in the church building on Sunday. This is a tragedy!

There are several things that I fear. Recently I visited an old lady in the retirement village where she now lives. She had a small room in which she lived and slept. On the walls she had hung her treasures. She had colourful pieces of tapestry which she had created when her eyesight was good. On one of her chairs there were several lovely porcelain dolls that she had made. She had many other items of knitting and sewing which she proudly showed me. Then she showed me her Bible which had a beautiful

46

leather cover on which she had impressed the picture of hands joined together in prayer.

After I had read the Scriptures and prayed with her we spent some time speaking of the goodness of God. Then with a great degree of difficulty she made a cup of tea. I tried to leave but she insisted that her minister should have afternoon tea. I felt very much at home with that gracious Christian woman.

When the time came for me to leave she said, 'Come and have a look at the scene from my balcony. It overlooks wonderful farming country.'

She opened the door leading to her balcony and as I walked through I became overwhelmed with fear. My face became flushed and I felt my legs tremble. Her balcony was on the third floor of the building and I am afraid of heights. When she asked me to look out over the farmlands I couldn't move forward to the railing. I leaned back against the wall and whispered my excuse: 'I can't look. I'm afraid of heights.' I had a quick glance round about and then retreated inside her room. I was so pleased eventually to get outside and have my feet on good solid earth.

I do not like plane travel. Val enjoys the trips on the plane. She sits near a window and looks down, saying to me, 'Look down there! Can you see …?' I just bury my head in a book or look at the back of the seat in front of me. My hands perspire and drops of sweat form on my face. All I can think of is that there is a small sheet of metal between me and the 10,000 metre fall to the ground. I don't like being in a lift for the same reason. I know what it is to be afraid of heights and move very carefully when my feet leave ground level.

There was a time when God's people and the heathen nations around them feared Jehovah (the LORD), the God of Israel. Today's reading speaks of the Israelites who were soon to enter and conquer the nations of Canaan. The spies had gone to the city of Jericho where they were met and protected by Rahab.

It was Rahab who told them that the people who inhabited Canaan were afraid of the people of Israel, because they feared the God of the Israelites. They had heard of the great miracles God had performed in Egypt. The Egyptian nation and their ruler, Pharaoh, had been humbled by the almighty power of God. Now the Canaanites saw the armies of Israel on their borders. They trembled because they had heard of the two great kings, Sihon and Og, who were overthrown by the power of the Lord. The people of Jericho knew that they probably would be conquered next. They trembled before the might of the God of Israel. He could not be defeated. The people in Jericho believed that their walls would not protect them on the day when the armies of Israel called on them. Rahab said that when the citizens of Jericho heard of Israel's victories, 'Our hearts melted; neither did there remain any more courage in anyone because of you, for the LORD your God, he is God in heaven above and on earth beneath' (Joshua 2:11).

The almighty God of Israel is our God, and sinners should fear him, for he has power to condemn them to eternal hell. On Judgement Day that is exactly what will happen to those who do not repent of their sins and believe in the Lord Jesus for salvation.

Our text tells us that 'Our God is a consuming fire.' This reminds us that we who are Christians should also fear God because he is our Lord, the uncreated Being who created us from the dust. He is our Redeemer who saved us from sins and we who belong to Christ should rejoice that we have the privilege of calling God 'Our Father'. We are not terrified of his presence in the same way as those who have not repented of their sins (see Revelation 6:15-17). However, he is still the almighty one. The holy, sinless angels of heaven bow in awe in his presence and cry out, 'Holy, holy, holy is the LORD of hosts; the whole earth is full of his glory!' (Isaiah 6:3). Too many professing Christians have forgotten the command of Scripture to all who love God (and those who have no interest in God): 'Fear God and keep his commandments...' (Ecclesiastes 12:13).

We must hold our God in awe and worship him with 'reverence and godly fear'. Let us all honour our loving, saving God and praise the Lord Jesus Christ for his life and death as the substitute for his people. May we tremble with a 'godly fear' as we gather for worship and ever praise almighty God for his wonderful salvation in Jesus Christ.

To think about

1. Discuss the two types of fear spoken of in the Scriptures.
2. What does it mean to 'honour God'?
3. How do Christians show others that they 'fear God'?

Theft is sin!

Read
● ● ● ● ● ● ● ● ● ● ● ● ● ● ● ● ● ● ●
Jeremiah 7:1-11

'You shall not steal'
(Exodus 20:15).

To steal another person's property is a wicked thing to do. Today people steal openly without any fear of the God whose law they are breaking.

During my time in the ministry the manse was beside the church building and facing a major road. Many people called asking for food and help. This was always given, but we had a difficulty when strangers arrived asking for money. One man asked for $5.00 which he said was to be the bus fare to get home. Later that day we saw him in a local park, half drunk, enjoying a bottle of wine which he had probably bought with our five dollars.

I decided that I would be more careful in future when asked for money. However, one man in a very expensive car called in after the banks had closed and asked for a loan of $100 to get him home. He seemed so sincere, even praising God and praying with me. He appeared genuine, but I took particular note of his car number-plate when he left with my money. In fact it turned out he was a thief, and my money was never returned. A policeman, who was a member of the congregation, investigated the whole matter, but no action could be taken. From that day onwards Val and I decided that no more money would be handed out to callers. The deacons helped genuine cases of need, but I was not caught out again.

Then a friend told me that one day a man called at his home with a ladder on one shoulder and a bag of tools over the other. This friend was a member of the air force, working in Malaysia. The caller said he was from the air-force home-maintenance company and had come to repair a large ceiling-fan.

Soon he was tinkering with the fan, but said, with a worried look on his face, that it needed to be returned to the workshop for repairs.

My friend said, 'I didn't know there was anything wrong with the fan. It was working OK last night.'

The workman, who seemed to know what he was talking about, replied, 'There's a problem with these fans and if they are not repaired you could have a fire.'

So the fan was pulled down and that was the last time they ever saw the fan, or the workman, who, they later discovered, had already visited the homes of several other air-force families and stolen electrical equipment.

Today theft is on the increase. Our homes are no longer safe from people who steal to buy drugs. We are forced to put special locks and burglar-proof fittings on the doors and windows of our homes to keep out unwelcome visitors. But if someone really wants to get into our homes and steal, it seems nothing can prevent it happening.

Thieves are despicable people! But what about you and me? Are we guilty of theft? I trust you don't go about stealing other people's property.

Our reading from Jeremiah contains an accusation from God that the covenant people of Israel were guilty of serious crimes. The prophet asks the question: 'Will you steal, murder, commit adultery, swear falsely, burn incense to Baal and walk after other gods whom you do not know…?'

Ask yourself the same question, 'Will I steal?'

I'm sure your answer will be: 'No! I do not steal!'

Good! However, do you always give to the Lord's work as you should? This applies not just to the money we give to the church, but to the time we devote to the Lord's service. Do we make time to read the Bible and pray? Do we spend time meditating upon God's law?

Many times we say, 'I don't have time!' We must make the time, not only to worship God, but to do the works God has called us to do. We are to help our neighbours by doing acts of kindness and showing love to them.

God challenges us to support gospel work. We read,

Will a man rob God?
Yet you have robbed me!
But you say,
'In what way have we robbed you?'
In tithes and offerings…
For you have robbed me…'

Then God issues a challenge to his people, Israel:

'Bring all the tithes into the storehouse,
That there may be food in my house,
And try me now in this,'
Says the LORD of hosts,

'If I will not open for you the windows of heaven
And pour out for you such a blessing
That there will not be room enough to receive it'

(Malachi 3:8-10).

We are to serve the Lord, not expecting a reward, but because we love him. We must never steal the property of another person as God will provide us with all we need in this life and blessings beyond our imagination in the life to come.

So let us all remember the commandment: 'You shall not steal.' May people be able to say of each one of my readers: 'That person can be trusted implicitly.' That will be the case if you are truly growing into the likeness of your Saviour. Trust God for all that you need and rejoice in all that he has given you.

To think about

1. Why do Christians obey the commandments of God? Read John 14:15 and 1 John 2:3-5.
2. Discuss some prayers that God has answered for you.
3. Why do Christians give to the work of the church? How do Christians determine how much they should give? Read 2 Corinthians 9:6-7.

Help! Let me in!

Read
Matthew 25:1-13

'So those that entered, male and female of all flesh, went in as God had commanded him; and the LORD shut him in' (Genesis 7:16).

Today's text is one that should be a comfort to Christians and fearful to those who are not interested in the Saviour. Noah had prepared that great ark, just as God had commanded. He had warned the people of that sinful generation that they all needed to repent of their sins and turn to God in obedience to his holy law.

Nevertheless, the people thought they knew better than Noah. They laughed at him while he and his family built the ark. Maybe some of them worked for Noah, cutting timber and driving in the nails. They were quite happy to take the pay that Noah gave them. But how they laughed behind his back! Others laughed in his face, mocking him as a silly old man who didn't know what he was doing. Those evil people loved their sinful ways and kept on sinning and despising God.

They should have known better. They would have known about the Garden of Eden and God's creation of Adam and Eve. They would also have heard of sin and of Adam being driven out of the garden with Eve, but probably thought it was just a legend. They didn't believe the story was true. They thought they knew better.

Then the day came when the ark was finished and all the animals were safe and secure in the rooms that had been built for them. Noah, Mrs Noah,

their three sons, Shem, Ham and Japheth, and their three wives entered the ark and God shut the door. Seven days later the rain fell! (Genesis 7:4).

God's small family of righteous people were shut in, which meant every-one else was shut out! Try to imagine how those people must have tried to climb up the side of the ark to find safety — but it was too late! The day of grace had passed.

Being locked out is an unpleasant experience. Some time ago an old deaf man invited a married couple I know to spend a holiday in his home. It overlooked the ocean and Mary and Graeme spent a very happy couple of weeks away from work. Each afternoon as the sun set they would sit on the small verandah and look out over the ocean. When they went to bed they listened to the sound of the waves crashing on the shore. They had a most enjoyable time.

All too soon their holiday was about to end. Only one more evening and night remained. So they bought a delicious Chinese meal and together sat on the verandah, eating their meal and watching the sun slowly sink below the horizon. Suddenly a gust of wind blew and the door onto the verandah slammed shut.

Mary jumped up and to her horror found the door was locked. There were no windows to climb through and the flat in which they were staying was on the second floor of the building.

'What are we going to do now?' Mary asked. 'I told you to put some-thing against the door to stop it blowing shut.'

'Well,' replied Graeme, 'it's too late now to worry about that. We'll call out and attract the attention of someone. They can get through the front door and open this one onto the verandah.'

They called out, but no one heard as the cars whizzed by and the waves roared. It seemed that they were marooned out there for the night. Then came the mosquitoes in their thousands.

At long last Graeme could stand it no longer. The mosquitoes were biting and Mary was complaining. 'All right,' said Graeme, picking up a big beach umbrella which was lying on the balcony, 'This is as good as a parachute. It's not far to the ground and nothing can go wrong. We'll be inside in no time.'

Graeme jumped only to discover that the umbrella quickly turned inside out. The loud scream he made as he fell, and the even louder one he made when he hit the ground, attracted the attention of the people in the ground-floor flat. Soon the ambulance arrived and Graeme was off to hospital with a broken leg — but the door was opened and Mary was safe inside, packing their belongings so she could go to the hospital to be with her husband. She wanted to be with him as he went to the operating theatre to have his badly broken leg set. Yes, to be locked out can be a fearful experience.

The parable we have read today is a frightening one because it is about people who thought they would have a home in the new creation. They were all waiting for the return of Christ, but when he came some were locked out — the door to heaven was closed to them.

These were people who read their Bibles and attended church, all the time believing they were Christians. They probably did many good deeds, helping people — *but...*! They were not born again and united to Christ by a living, God-given faith. They had never truly repented of their sins and now for them it was all too late. Christ had returned and gathered his people to himself, and all the rest were locked out. 'Lord, Lord, open to us!' they cried out but Christ replied, 'I do not know you!'

Now where do you stand this day in spiritual things? What is your relationship to Christ? Can you say with the apostle Paul, 'I live by faith in the Son of God, who loved me and gave himself for me'? (Galatians 2:20).

May the day come when we are all gathered together before the throne of God to glorify Christ and enjoy him for ever. May none who read these words be among those who have the door to heaven closed in their faces.

To think about

1. When is it that Christ will return? How do you know this?
2. List five things that will happen when Christ returns to earth a second time.
3. Where and what is heaven?
4. List five signs that would convince you that a person is a Christian.

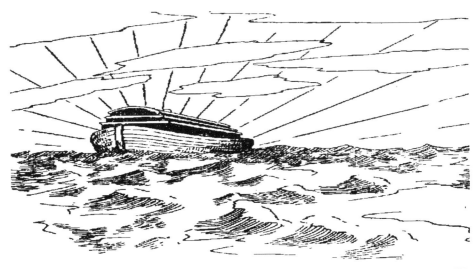

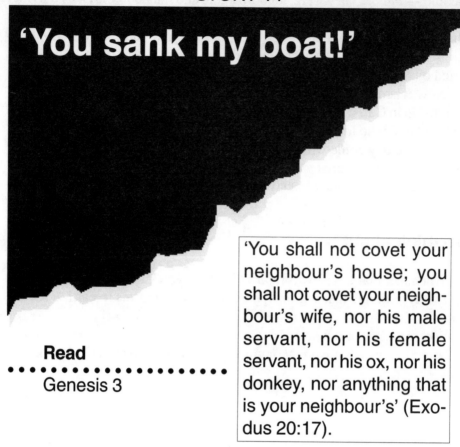

'You sank my boat!'

'You shall not covet your neighbour's house; you shall not covet your neighbour's wife, nor his male servant, nor his female servant, nor his ox, nor his donkey, nor anything that is your neighbour's' (Exodus 20:17).

Read
• • • • • • • • • • • • • • • • • • • •
Genesis 3

The tenth commandment is a warning that we are not to lust after another person's possessions. This sin starts in the mind when our eyes see something we want more than anything else. Sometimes we never tell anyone of these thoughts, but they are sinful because God has commanded us to be satisfied with all he has given us. This does not mean that the sin of coveting remains hidden for ever, because God can see into our hearts and minds and knows our every thought.

Sometimes we are not satisfied with just thinking about the other person's possessions, but try to get them for ourselves by wicked means.

Our reading is about Adam and Eve in the Garden of Eden. They were given a special commandment by God: 'Everything in the garden is yours, except the fruit on the tree of the knowledge of good and evil.' Adam and Eve enjoyed living in that perfect garden that God had created for them, until Eve looked at the forbidden fruit. When she saw 'that the tree was good for food, that it was pleasant to the eyes, and a tree desirable to make one wise, she took of its fruit and ate'.

Eve wanted that piece of fruit for herself, even though it was not hers. She coveted that fruit! By that sinful act she plunged the whole world into

58

sin and chaos. That one act resulted in the death of every person who has ever lived except Elijah and Enoch. That one act resulted in the creation of hell to receive all unrepentant sinners.

In Jerusalem one day King David looked out from his palace and saw the beautiful Bathsheba taking a bath on the roof of her home (2 Samuel 11). At once David coveted another man's wife and we know of the terrible sin that followed. He saw a woman who was not his, coveted her and then stole her for himself. It was Nathan who told King David the parable about the rich man who when he had visitors didn't want to kill one of his own sheep to cook for the meal. He had seen a poor man's sheep and decided he wanted it for the meal. He saw, he coveted and he stole.

Now when we read these stories we probably think to ourselves how wicked those people were and that we would not do such bad things. We probably say to ourselves, 'I might think about something I want, but would never hurt anyone by taking it from them.'

The Bible tells us: 'For out of the heart proceed evil thoughts, murders, adulteries, fornications, thefts, false witness, blasphemies' (Matthew 15:19). As we all have sinful hearts we must be on guard all the time so that we do not sin.

When John and I were young we lived an exciting life on our parents' farm. We had so many wonderful things to do that we were always busy. We swam in the river, fished in it and rowed the family boat about on it. We also had toy boats which we sailed about in a pool of water. Many of our boats were home-made and they usually capsized, filled with water and sank to the bottom of the pool or stream.

One time we were each given a toy boat which was so much better than anything we had ever made. When the wind blew we would set the sails and let the small ships make their way across the pool. Then we would fetch them and do it all again. However, there was one thing I didn't like about the sailing races and it was that John's boat always won the race. His boat was better than mine! I also thought his boat was painted with brighter paint and had bigger sails.

Often I thought to myself, 'If only I had been given John's boat and he had mine I'd be really happy.' But this could never be and I often hoped his boat would capsize and sink to the bottom. Then my boat would be victorious!

Sometimes as the tiny ships made their way across the pool we would toss lumps of earth into the water near them and watch them bump up and down through the small waves we had made. That always made the race more exciting, and sometimes I thought my boat would win. But it never happened and I was always unhappy. Sometimes I thought of hiding John's boat and then I would be happy.

One day my jealous thoughts devised a plan to get rid of my brother's boat. We walked down to the dam, pleased with the breeze that was just right for a sailing race. However, I intended to put a stop to John's boat always being the winner.

The boats slowly made their way away from the edge of the pool and I suggested we throw some large lumps of earth near them to make really big waves. At first all went well, but I had a plan! I picked up a rather large rock and with much more force than usual and with good aim I threw it straight at John's boat. The rock landed just where I intended — right on the deck! The boat's mast split, the hull broke in two and she capsized and began to disappear below the surface of the water.

Maybe John saw the smirk on my face, but as he shouted out, 'You sank my boat!' I turned and ran for the house with John hard on my heels. That was the end of our sailing races and I never saw my boat again. I had coveted John's sailing boat and then sinfully destroyed what was not mine, because I couldn't have it for myself.

Have you ever thought such wicked thoughts? Have you ever stolen, or spoilt, what was not yours, simply because you wanted the thing for yourself? Coveting is a sin that is found in many places in the Scriptures. It was Satan who in heaven coveted God's throne and power. In his mind he thought:

I will ascend into heaven,
I will exalt my throne above the stars of God;
I will also sit on the mount of the congregation...
I will ascend above the heights of the clouds,
I will be like the Most High

(Isaiah 14:13-14).

That sin was the start of all our problems!

May we ever enjoy and be satisfied with all that God has given us and never become so dissatisfied that we fall into sin by taking what is not ours.

We must ever be on guard against advertisers who tell us that we should not be satisfied with what we have, but constantly encourage us to buy things that we do not really need. We need to remember the words found in James 1:14: 'But each one is tempted when he is drawn away by his own desires and enticed. Then, when desire has conceived, it gives birth to sin; and when it is full-grown, brings forth death.'

To think about

1. Make a list of five things other people have that you would like.
2. How can you obtain those things without sinning?
3. Which commandments can coveting cause us to break?

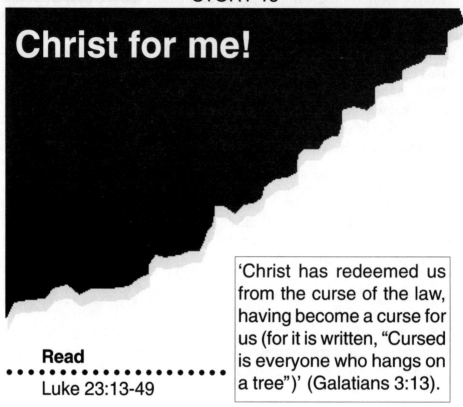

Christ for me!

Read
• • • • • • • • • • • • • • • • • • • •
Luke 23:13-49

'Christ has redeemed us from the curse of the law, having become a curse for us (for it is written, "Cursed is everyone who hangs on a tree")' (Galatians 3:13).

In our reading of the Bible passage from Luke I am sure you noticed the horrendous treatment that our Saviour, the Lord Jesus Christ, received from those cruel soldiers as they whipped him. They mocked him, dressing him in the clothes of a king, while treating him as a common criminal. They hated Christ because they hated the Jews and knew that by killing the one who claimed to be the 'King of the Jews' they ridiculed the Jewish nation.

The hours before the crucifixion and those long, distressing hours when Christ hung upon the cross are the time when the greatest blasphemy against God in the history of this world was carried out. The sinful creation was in the act of killing the holy Creator.

Christians all down the ages have been ashamed of what those cruel, heartless men and women did that day in Jerusalem. We weep tears of sorrow because our Lord was so shamefully treated.

But there was something much worse happening that day, as cruel, sinful men were about to crucify Christ — it was the day when Christ became sin for his people. On the cross Christ, my substitute, was bearing my sins. He hung upon the cross suffering hell in my place — and yours, if you are a believer. The one who was pouring out his anger upon Christ was God, Christ's heavenly Father.

The doctrine of substitution is hard for some people to accept, but the truth is that Christ lived a life of perfect obedience and accepted the punishment of God for sin on behalf of his sinful people.

Many years ago I used to travel on a bus to attend secondary school. Sad to say, there were days when the behaviour of the young people — including myself — was not very good. We messed around on the bus. The bus conductor was very upset one day by some silly behaviour and on that occasion I happened to be an innocent bystander, along with my friend who sat on the seat beside me.

A secondary-school girl grabbed the conductor's whistle and threw it towards the back of the bus. When the poor fellow struggled through the children to get his whistle it was thrown to someone else. After a few minutes the conductor became furious and shouted out that he wanted his whistle returned or someone would be ordered off the bus.

When the whistle was next thrown it hit the boy beside me on the shoulder and fell to the floor of the bus. As the conductor bent down to pick up his property one of the girls flicked him on the back. He jumped up, red in the face and furious.

My friend, realizing that something violent was about to happen, quietly said, 'I didn't do it.' Then he stepped between the girls who were to blame and the angry conductor in order to protect them from his anger. What happened next was a frightening experience for everyone and some weeks later I was summoned to appear in court and give evidence about the events. However, the point we need to note here is that by putting himself between the bus conductor and the girls, my friend took the punishment in the place of the youngsters who were responsible for causing the trouble.

On the cross Christ accepted the responsibility for the sins of his people and suffered dreadfully at the hands of those wicked Romans and Jews.

However, that was not the worst aspect of the punishment he received. Our text reminds us that Jesus Christ became 'a curse for us'. As he hung upon the cross the Father suspended that perfect unity that existed with his Son. For a short period of time something took place that had never happened before, nor will ever occur again — Christ became sin for his people. Every sin his people ever committed was placed on him and God turned his face away from his Son. That is why Christ cried out in agony, 'My God, my God, why have you forsaken me?' That is hell — to be forsaken by God. Christ was forsaken so that his people might never be forsaken.

There on Calvary a great transaction took place: my sins were placed upon Christ and his perfect righteousness was put to my account. Praise God for what happened that day, for through Christ's suffering his people are saved.

All who belong to Christ rejoice and worship him in the words of the psalmist:

Enter into his gates with thanksgiving,
And into his courts with praise.
Be thankful to him, and bless his name.
For the Lord is good;
His mercy is everlasting,
And his truth endures to all generations

(Psalm 100:4-5).

Thank God for our wonderful Saviour!

To think about

1. What sign was placed upon Christ's cross? Why did the Romans put that sign on the cross? Read John 19:19-22.
2. Why was Christ forsaken by his Father?
3. What is hell?
4. How are sinners saved? Read Acts 16:31.

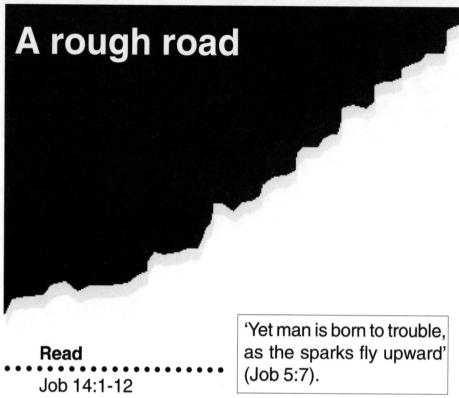

A rough road

Read
• • • • • • • • • • • • • • • • • • • •
Job 14:1-12

'Yet man is born to trouble,
as the sparks fly upward'
(Job 5:7).

There is no doubt that life can be very difficult and heart-breaking for some people, while others seem to enjoy their days and die a peaceful death. Events during the last couple of days have once again reminded me of the tragedy of sin that has ruined human existence. The only thing that makes life bearable for many people is the loving-kindness of God as seen in their saving faith in Christ.

Someone once told me that the pathway of life was a 'bed of roses'. My reply to that was: 'The pathway of roses still has a lot of thorns.' A friend, who is also an elder of a congregation, has just received the news that he has a serious type of cancer. Another elder I know quite well has had a stroke which has left him very ill indeed. A close friend of my wife recently found herself alone because her husband deserted the family. Several of her children are mixed up in various kinds of trouble. She is totally heart-broken and has not attended church for some time. All of these people are suffering a great deal of hurt. Job's words are so true: 'Yet man is born to trouble, as the sparks fly upward.'

Sometimes the fire burns softly and there are few, if any, sparks, while at other times, when the wind blows, or when you start poking it with a stick, sparks fly about everywhere. Life is like that. Most people have times when life is pleasant, but also experience hard, distressing times.

God had greatly blessed Job and his life was one of praise to God for all his wonderful gifts. However, we know what Job did not know — that Satan was the cause of all his troubles.

We may think that things are going badly for us, but let us stop for a moment and think about Job. His sons and daughters were all killed, his possessions were all stolen or destroyed, and his wife urged him to 'Curse God and die!' (Job 2:9). When his friends visited him they put the blame for his troubles upon his own shoulders, saying that God was punishing him for his sinfulness. So distressed was Job that he cried out, 'Why did I not die at birth? Why did I not perish when I came from the womb?' (Job 3:11). Job was feeling the thorns which are to be found along life's pathway!

I visited a man whose life had become very difficult. He owned a farm and was building a roadway from the main road to a spot where one day he hoped to build a house. His farm road was like the pathway of life. My car, which is low to the ground, scraped and bumped along on the rough track. When I came to an incline which he was building it was so steep the car found difficulty in making it up the slope. Then it was down again to a perfectly flat stretch of road. That was the easy part! I next had to drive up a hill made up of soft dirt which he had just dumped. I knew the car would

never make it, but the man called out, 'Go on, Jim! You can do it!' However, my car couldn't do it — even if I could! — and was soon bogged down.

With the man's help the car was eventually pushed out of the soft soil and I continued my journey to the end of the road, where he told me of his difficulties and troubles. He had given up going to church and was no longer reading his Bible — in fact he had given his Bible away. Life had really knocked him flat.

I had with me a friend who also was a pastor and, out there in the bush, beside his old truck loaded with sand and surrounded by biting mosquitoes in their millions, my pastor friend opened the Word of God and read Psalm 23. He and I both spoke to the man about the grace of God and the suffering of the Lord Jesus in the place of his people. Then we offered up prayer to the God of all grace, with the result that the man we had come to visit opened his wallet and gave me money to buy him the best Bible I could. He promised to come to church on the Lord's Day.

Then came the rough ride along his track to get back onto the main road. Life is like that road. There are many rough patches and then some smooth sections. All the time we need to understand that we have a Saviour who knows how we feel when troubles arise. Christ was 'made like his brethren, that he might be a merciful and faithful High Priest in things pertaining to God, to make propitiation for the sins of the people... For in that he himself has suffered, being tempted, he is able to aid those who are tempted.' 'For we do not have a High Priest who cannot sympathize with our weaknesses, but was in all points tempted as we are, yet without sin. Let us therefore come boldly to the throne of grace, that we may obtain mercy and find grace to help in time of need' (Hebrews 2:17-18; 4:15-16).

When troubles come we should not close our Bibles and give up attending worship, as if God were responsible for our difficulties. We should read our Bibles and pray, always walking closely with the Lord Jesus.

Our Saviour knows what we are going through. He experienced heartache and distress as well as physical torment. He experienced the sense of loss of fellowship with his Father, which was truly hell.

A writer once said something like this: 'God whispers to us when life is easy and shouts to us in our troubles.' When life is going along easily we so often tend to forget God. It is in the hard times that we cry to God for help. It is when the world turns against us that we walk closely with Christ, because he understands our problems and is there to give help. It is the God of peace who will grant us his peace.

Faithfulness to Christ and love of God will have their reward on that day when the world comes to an end and we stand before the throne of Christ to hear his words of welcome: 'Well done, good and faithful servant. You have been faithful when the roadway of life was difficult. Now enter into the rest I have prepared for you.'

To think about

1. Read Psalm 73 and talk about the meaning that comes from the words of the psalmist.
2. Hard times are sure to come your way. How are you going to cope in those situations?
3. What can you do to help people experiencing difficulties?
4. Why could the psalmist say, 'It is good for me that I have been afflicted, that I may learn your statutes'? (Psalm 119:71).

Where's the key?

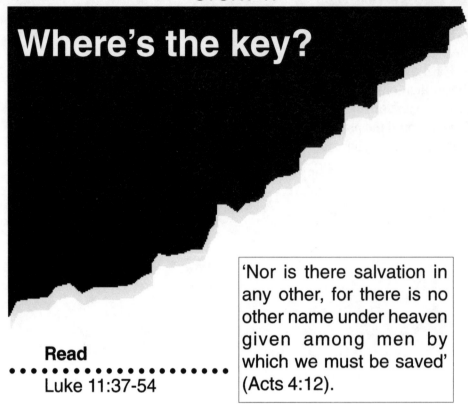

Read
• • • • • • • • • • • • • • • • • • • •
Luke 11:37-54

'Nor is there salvation in any other, for there is no other name under heaven given among men by which we must be saved' (Acts 4:12).

Keys have become a very important part of our modern life. Today people seem to be carrying more keys in their pockets or bags than ever before. I have often seen people carrying a bunch of keys hanging from a belt.

Keys are useful for opening locked doors and for locking doors securely. We find the word 'key' or 'keys' mentioned several times in the Scriptures.

Some time ago several Australian cricketers who had performed very well were given a parade through the streets of Sydney. When they met the Lord Mayor he presented them with the key to the city.

Now I have travelled many times through the city of Sydney and never once did I need a key. The roads had no blockades of any kind. However, cities were not always like they are today. There was a time when large towns and cities were surrounded by strong walls to keep out the enemy. Each city had one or two gates through which all travellers had to pass. Each morning someone unlocked the city gates so that people could come and go. If a traveller arrived during the night when the gate was securely shut he may have found it difficult to get the watchman on duty out of bed to unlock the gate and let him through. To receive the key to the city meant you were a trusted and honoured person who had the authority to pass through the city gates at any time of the day or night without disturbing the sleep of the gatekeeper.

One day a friend of mine found himself unable to get into the house where he was staying. He had recently arrived from Scotland and didn't know what to do. In desperation he tried his car keys but they proved to be useless. Then he tried the key to his suitcase but that was too small. He even asked for help from the next-door neighbour, but without success. Yes, Sam was locked out. Finally he had to drive to the home of the owner of the house and borrow another set of keys. At last he was able to get into the house.

There is a home being prepared by the Lord Jesus Christ for his people. Many people hope that one day they will be able to enter through those heavenly doors and live with Christ for ever.

In the book of Revelation we have a wonderful description of the heavenly city, which has twelve gates (Revelation 21:12). But how are people to gain entry to heaven through one of those twelve gates?

Some people claim that they have the key of 'good works' — they have helped many people and because of this they believe God will open heaven's door and allow them in. But that is not so! Good works will get no one through those heavenly doors.

Others will say, 'I've attended church. I've read my Bible. I've prayed...' However, all of those keys put together will not open the doors of heaven. Religion does not save sinners. There is only one key to heaven, and that key has been provided by God, the owner of the heavenly city.

The key to heaven is God's one and only Son, the Lord Jesus Christ. Our text puts it very plainly: 'Nor is there salvation in any other, for there is no other name under heaven given among men by which we must be saved.'

Jesus himself said, 'I am the way, the truth, and the life. No one comes to the Father except through me' (John 14:6). Jesus Christ is the only key to open the door of heaven. Isn't that wonderful? God himself has provided the way into his kingdom.

When death takes you from this earth it is Christ who will unlock heaven's doors and bid you welcome, if you have faith in him. Do you know him as your Lord and Saviour?

Today's reading is about the Pharisees and the lawyers who taught the people about the false keys to heaven. Of them Christ said, 'Woe to you lawyers! For you have taken away the key of knowledge. You did not enter in yourselves, and those who were entering in you hindered' (Luke 11:52).

Read your Bible, for there you will find Christ, the key to salvation and eternal life. He is not only the key, but also the door through which his people must pass (John 10:7).

To think about

1. Today's reading speaks of Abel. Who was Abel and why is he mentioned in this passage of Scripture?

2. Who were the Pharisees?

3. What key were the Pharisees expecting to use to open heaven's gates? Why was this key sure to be a failure?

A rude awakening

Read
Isaiah 40:9-26

'Behold, the Lord GOD shall come with a strong hand, and his arm shall rule for him; behold, his reward is with him, and his work before him. He will feed his flock like a shepherd; he will gather the lambs with his arm, and carry them in his bosom, and gently lead those who are with young' (Isaiah 40:10-11).

There are many sides to the character of any person. If I look closely at myself I see someone who can be very serious at times yet very light-hearted at others. I can weep and smile; I can be gentle on occasions, and strong when I need to be. I'm sure that most of us are like this. We are all a mixture of different characteristics. The same is true of our God.

The text we have for today is one that thrills my heart as it speaks of my God who is all-powerful and yet very gentle. He rules the world in righteousness, disciplining, or chastening, his people when necessary and punishing the wicked. He is also a God of love and mercy, yet a God who in holy anger sends unrepentant sinners to hell.

When we study the character of our God we need to remember that there are many sides to his character. The *Larger Catechism (Westminster Confession of Faith)* describes God in the following words: 'God is a spirit, in and of himself infinite in being, glory, blessedness, and perfection; all-sufficient, eternal, unchangeable, incomprehensible, everywhere present, almighty, knowing all things, most wise, most holy, most just, most merciful and gracious, long-suffering, and abundant in goodness and truth' (answer to question 7).

A friend of mine once discovered that his pet cat, which he loved, was not just a lovely placid ball of fluff. The cat would jump up on his lap, curl up and purr herself to sleep. On other occasions she would play with his shoelaces, chase a piece of wool and be his very best friend. Never once had the cat clawed him. He just knew one aspect of his pet's nature — sweetness, love and softness. However, one night he discovered there was another side to his pet's character.

Peter's cat usually slept inside the house on a comfortable chair, but one night decided she would sleep under his bed. All was quiet. Nothing stirred. But the cat had one eye open. Peter said it was in the early hours of the morning when he turned over in bed and his foot poked out from under the sheet and blanket. For some reason the cat attacked his protruding toes.

Peter couldn't help laughing when telling me of the incident. 'I was sound asleep,' he said, 'when suddenly I had the most shocking pain in my foot. It felt as if a broken piece of glass was scratching me. I couldn't believe what was happening. I gave a sudden cry for help. Judy [his wife] woke up and grabbed me, asking if I was having a nightmare. However, it was no nightmare! Quickly I switched on the light and found blood dripping from my foot. I still didn't understand what had happened, until that pet cat crept out from under the bed.'

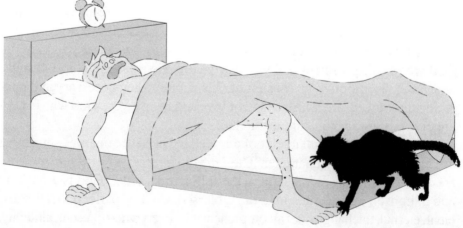

Peter now saw another side to the character of his affectionate pet cat. There was a vicious streak in her personality. Peter hobbled out of bed, patched up his sore toe and when he returned to bed there was the cat curled up in the warm spot where he had been sleeping. I think it was then that the cat found out for the first time what it was like to sleep outside the house in the cold air!

Today there are many people who teach and believe that our God is just all love. After all, the Bible says, 'God is love' (1 John 4:8). They fail to understand that God is holy and just in all his ways. The psalmist adds another aspect of God's nature: 'God is a just judge, and God is angry with the wicked every day' (Psalm 7:11).

Some think that everyone will be forgiven and find a home in heaven, but this is not so, as we discover in Exodus 34:6-7, where we read of God's character, '… The LORD, the LORD God, merciful and gracious, longsuffering, and abounding in goodness and truth, keeping mercy for thousands, forgiving iniquity and transgression and sin, by no means clearing the guilty…' Our God hates sin and will not spare the guilty. However, he loves a vast number of people whom no one can count and these will all come to faith in the Lord Jesus Christ. These, and these alone, will eternally enjoy the new creation.

Our God is a 'jealous' God — jealous of his good name and jealous of his people. He is also a forgiving God and a God of grace. May everyone who reads these words come to know Christ, who is both God and man in the one person, and love him faithfully throughout their lives.

To think about

1. What does the Scripture mean when it says, 'God is love'? (1 John 4:8).
2. God is a 'jealous' God. Of what is God jealous?
3. What does the catechism mean when it says that God is 'all-sufficient'?

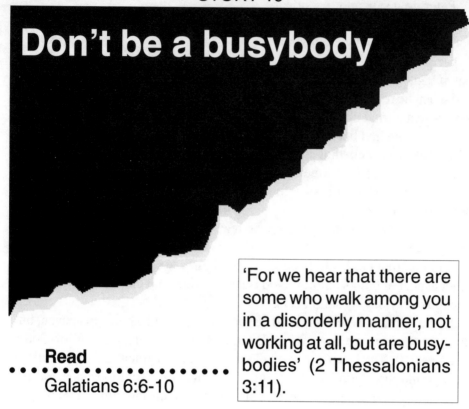

Don't be a busybody

'For we hear that there are some who walk among you in a disorderly manner, not working at all, but are busybodies' (2 Thessalonians 3:11).

Read
• •
Galatians 6:6-10

Busybodies are not popular people. In some parts of the world they are called 'stickybeaks' because they poke their noses into other people's business to satisfy their curiosity. They make it their business to find out all they can about others, then get their information confused, or add to it, and pass on to others what is not always true. This damages a person's character and God has something to say to busybodies because such people are sinning.

The church at Thessalonica had among their number professing Christian people who were not working. They came to borrow food from others who had a job, while they themselves didn't want to work even though jobs were available. Of course they had spare time — too much spare time — and used it to spy on other people so they could talk about them. They were stickybeaks and busybodies. When Paul wrote to Timothy he warned him about the young widows who had time on their hands: 'And besides they learn to be idle, wandering about from house to house, and not only idle but also gossips and busybodies, saying things which they ought not' (1 Timothy 5:13).

I trust that you are not a busybody.

My Wags is a busybody and causes us a lot of difficulty with this bad habit. When he was growing up I taught him to stand on his back legs and look out through the low bay window of our bedroom. Val would stand

outside while I held him up so he could see her. It wasn't long before he would run to the window when he heard her outside and peer out to see what was happening. I would then say, 'Good on you, Wags!' Val and I would laugh at our dog who could look out through the window. He looked so cute!

It wasn't long before Wags began to peer out of the window all by himself at every noise he heard. When a car came near he would run to the window and, standing on his toes, would watch what was happening. If he heard a cat or dog he would look out and start barking. Of course Val and I thought our intelligent little dog was wonderful. He knew everything that was going on outside. If he recognized the sound of our car, or Val walking by, he didn't run to the window, but instead raced to the front door to greet her. However, if a bird landed on the verandah he was there standing on his toes and barking at the bird to order it off.

Then we discovered that his claws had torn the lace curtain. However, we excused Wags as he was our special little dog. He sleeps on a bean bag beside our bed and now wakes up at the slightest noise — usually in the middle of the night — and races to the window where he barks at the top of his voice — although the night a burglar came and stole our garden hose he slept very soundly and didn't move!

Wags has become a very nosy little dog. When he sees people riding bikes past the house he barks furiously at them through the window and then races through the house to get to the gate so he can bark at them face to face. Val had to replace the lace curtains and we are now trying to retrain Wags to just look and keep quiet.

Our reading reminds us that as Christians we must be concerned with the well-being of others. We must discover those in need so that we may help them. But there

are too many people who are busybodies, who, when they hear a rumour about someone else, broadcast it far and wide, causing hurt to the person concerned. Christian love does not act that way. Christian love 'thinks no evil; does not rejoice in iniquity, but rejoices in the truth' (1 Corinthians 13:5-6).

May we be those who always help others without hurting them. Let none of us be gossips, taking pleasure in the difficulties or sins of other people, but let us do good to everyone, especially to those who are our Christian brothers and sisters.

To think about

1. What is Christian love? Read 1 Corinthians 13:4-8.
2. What is a 'stickybeak'?
3. We read in 1 Peter 4:8: 'Love will cover a multitude of sins.' What does this mean?
4. Look up and discuss one of the following proverbs — Proverbs 11:13; 20:19; 26:20.

It is all true

Read
• • • • • • • • • • • • • • • • • • •
Matthew 13:10-17

'It has been given to you to know the mysteries of the kingdom of heaven' (Matthew 13:11).

There are places in the Scriptures where we simply do not fully understand what Christ is saying. Words are written that are hard to comprehend and today's reading is such a passage. Many people ask when they read these words, 'Why would Christ deliberately speak in parables so that people cannot understand the truth of what he was saying?'

Unconverted people don't understand the spiritual truths which we speak. They have no true understanding of sin, or of how it grieves a holy God. To speak of a Saviour, the need of forgiveness and eternal life is like speaking in a foreign language to them. They cannot comprehend the truth.

When I was young I had a friend who was totally deaf from birth, which meant he could not speak correctly as he had never heard anyone else speak. I heard sounds he never heard. On one occasion when we were playing by the roadside a car rounded the corner travelling at a fast speed. The horn blew and I jumped out of the way, but Henry narrowly escaped being injured. He didn't hear the sound of the horn and it was only the quick action of the driver that saved his life. A warning sound had been made but Henry didn't hear.

Henry! Look out!

A similar situation occurred at school with a blind girl. She could not see the danger of an electric cord that had not been turned off. When Mary touched it she was fortunate to receive only a mild shock.

She couldn't see the sun and it was impossible to describe the sun to her in a way she could understand. There were so many other things she could not visualize, no matter what we said.

Both people needed help in order to understand the world about them. Henry needed hearing and Mary needed sight.

In today's reading Jesus spoke of people who could not understand the truth of what he said, even though they could hear his words. Others saw Christ and the miracles he performed, yet couldn't see the wonder of the salvation freely available to all who trusted themselves to him.

These words from the Scriptures which we read tell of a great mystery. Christ said he spoke in parables so that those who heard the words, and no doubt enjoyed the story, could not understand the truth he taught. Without a dramatic change in their understanding they would go through their lives not knowing the way of salvation. This was God's judgement upon his people, especially the Pharisees, because of their unbelief.

When Nicodemus came to Jesus one night (John 3:1-2) he wanted to learn about Christ and find out what he was teaching. Jesus told him plainly that he first of all needed this change in his life. He said, 'Most assuredly, I say to you, unless one is born again, he cannot see the kingdom of God' (John 3:3).

Sinners are all blind and deaf to the truth of God's Word. They must be born again before they are able to understand and obey Christ's command to repent of their sins and trust themselves to him for salvation.

So what about you? Are you still spiritually blind, or do you understand the truth concerning the Lord Jesus? Are you able to say of Christ with the apostle Peter, 'You are the Christ, the Son of the living God'? (Matthew 16:16). If this is true of you it means God has revealed the mystery to you: 'Flesh and blood has not revealed this to you, but my Father who is in heaven' (Matthew 16:17).

Our passage also plainly teaches us that God has a chosen people who will understand the truth of Christ's words. There are others who will live in their sins and die in their sins because they do not understand the truth of God's Word. The apostle Paul wrote, 'But the natural man does not receive the things of the Spirit of God, for they are foolishness to him; nor can he know them, because they are spiritually discerned' (1 Corinthians 2:14).

Where do you stand today? Always remember that Christ continues to invite sinners to himself that they may be saved. Today is indeed the day of grace!

To think about

1. What does it mean 'to be born again'?
2. How can you tell if a person is 'born again'?
3. Why did Christ speak so often using parables?

Freedom at last

Read
• • • • • • • • • • • • • • • • • • • •
John 8:30-36

'And having been set free from sin, you became slaves of righteousness' (Romans 6:18).

Slavery is a tragic blot upon human history. It is sad to think of people being bought and sold as if they were nothing more than animals. Slavery still exists today in some parts of the world and this is a shocking waste of human life! Some people cannot make decisions concerning their own future because they are the property of someone else.

For a moment, try to imagine yourself as being a slave. You are living in an old hut with ragged clothing and very little furniture. Your food is just very plain. Because you are a slave no one has bothered to teach you to read or write. You have no books, no TV, and no spare time to do as you please.

When you have had your breakfast you go out and work — and work, and work! If you are not working hard all the time the overseer gives you a taste of the whip he always carries with him. When night comes, you have a little food and then fall asleep because you are so tired. And every day is the same — work, work, work! There are no holidays in the future — just work!

In the Old Testament you can read of the Israelites who were slaves in Egypt. Life for them increasingly became little more than misery and work! (Read Exodus 1:8-14). However, God came to their rescue, sending them Moses who would lead them from the land of slavery.

I feel so sorry for the way the African slaves were treated by their white slave-traders. They were stolen from their homeland and taken to the New World — the Americas — where they became slaves, working on the plantations. Their treatment was barbaric. Some were thrown overboard by the captain of the transport ship if a British warship appeared on the horizon. Britain outlawed slavery and tried to police the seas in an effort to prevent the slave trade continuing. When a slave-ship's captain saw the British warship coming he had
the slaves chained together and pushed overboard. What cruelty! We must thank God for the work of men such as William Wilberforce who brought about changes in British law which outlawed slavery throughout the British Empire. We should also thank God for the great President of the USA, Abraham Lincoln, who worked so hard to bring slavery in the USA to an end.

I can assure you that I have no wish to be a slave — to be the personal possession of any other human being. If I were a slave I know I would be trying to escape from my owner.

And what about you? Would you like to be a slave? I'm sure your answer is, 'No!'

However, the truth is that every one of us is a slave to sin until God intervenes. Spiritual freedom is only found in Christ. Until the Holy Spirit brings about the new birth we are members of Satan's kingdom and slaves to his cruel rule. The apostle Paul told the sad truth when he wrote, 'You were slaves of sin' (Romans 6:20).

Being a slave to sin means that your first interest is yourself and the world of pleasure. It means that you are not able to serve God with a heart of love towards the Lord Jesus Christ. It means that you love your sins and have no desire to be holy. Satan's slaves don't want to worship God and glorify the Lord Jesus Christ.

Abraham Lincoln

A slave could be freed if some kind person purchased him and then released him. This is exactly what Jesus Christ did for his people. He paid the price of their freedom. Paul wrote, 'For you were bought at a price,' and this means that no longer do we own ourselves — nor does Satan (1 Corinthians 6:19-20). The great truth is that having been redeemed we belong to God.

Believers have been 'set free from sin, and … become slaves of God' (Romans 6:22). Being set free from the power of sin means we now are free to worship and serve God. Instead of serving sin we now serve Christ by living a life of righteousness.

We love God's law and by his grace live a life of obedience to him. When we fail it grieves us and we confess our sinfulness asking for forgiveness. And — praise be to God! — he forgives his people when they repent of their sins.

Sin does not rule in the life of Christ's people. We are set free, and for this we must praise God and give thanks to the Lord Jesus for redeeming us.

None of us could pay the price for our freedom from sin's dominion, but Jesus did this when he came into the world. First, he lived a life of perfect obedience to his Father; and, secondly, he was punished in the place of his people. Our salvation is all of God through the work of the Lord Jesus. All Christians should continually praise God for their wonderful salvation. No longer are they members of Satan's kingdom. We read a wonderful truth, written by the apostle Paul: 'He [God] has delivered us from the power of darkness and [brought] us into the kingdom of the Son of his love, in whom we have redemption through his blood, the forgiveness of sins' (Colossians 1:13-14).

Paul also wrote, 'The wages of sin is death, but the gift of God is eternal life in Christ Jesus our Lord' (Romans 6:23).

True spiritual freedom is found in Jesus Christ: 'If the Son makes you free, you shall be free indeed' (John 8:36). Have you found this freedom? If so, then Paul's words speak of you: 'Therefore you are no longer a slave but a son, and if a son, then an heir of God through Christ' (Galatians 4:7).

To think about

1. In what way are sinners slaves to Satan?
2. In what way is it pleasant to be a 'slave' of the Lord Jesus?
3. Our text indicates that Christians are 'slaves to righteousness'. What is 'righteousness'?

Death — a curse!

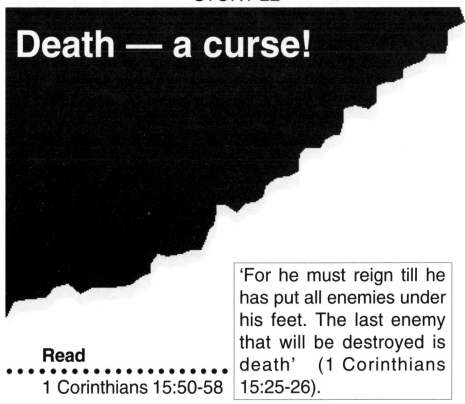

'For he must reign till he has put all enemies under his feet. The last enemy that will be destroyed is death' (1 Corinthians 15:25-26).

Death is an enemy which must be faced by every person born into this world. In the world's history only two people have passed out of this world without dying. Those two were Enoch and Elijah, both great servants of God. The only others who will not die are the ones living at the time when Christ returns and brings time and history to an end.

Death is a time of parting when we leave behind those people we love and all the things we have treasured. It also means we leave behind the

bodies in which we lived on earth. While the person's spirit has returned 'to God who gave it' (Ecclesiastes 12:7) the body is decaying and returning to the dust from which it was formed.

Yes, death is our enemy! However, the Scriptures speak of a better home for all who love the Lord Jesus. That home is heaven and of that place we read, 'And God will wipe away every tear from their eyes; there shall be no more death, nor sorrow, nor crying. There shall be no more pain, for the former things have passed away' (Revelation 21:4).

No more death! And why is this? The answer is simple: there is no sin. Sin pays wages — both physical and spiritual death.

There is, then, for the Christian another way to look at death. It is not just a time of parting — of leaving behind our families and so many things we value. It is a time of going home.

When I have been away from home I always have a longing in my heart to go home. When the day arrives for returning I know my heart beats faster. The closer I get to home, the more excited I feel. Recently I spent ten days away and I marked off the days as they passed. When I drove up the driveway at about 11 p.m. I could hear Wags barking at the top of his voice. He recognized the car. Then out came Val and Wags. I knew I was home because Val put her arms about me and gave me a 'welcome home' kiss, while Wags barked and jumped up my leg in order to attract my attention.

Death is 'going home' and that is how Christians should look at it. It is going home to be with God, to be with the Lord Jesus Christ. As Christians we love Jesus, our Saviour, and there should be a longing in our hearts to be with him. When the end of life draws near let our minds and hearts be filled with the wonder of 'going home'.

Recently a Christian couple were told that the husband had leukaemia. This was a shock to them both and several weeks later they learnt that the treatment was not working. When they asked what would be the outcome the doctor replied that death would soon follow. This Christian couple were devoted to Christ, which meant the husband could face his death with a true joy in his heart. Sure, he was leaving behind the wife and family he loved, but he was secure in the knowledge that he soon would be with the one who loved him with a far greater love than any human being — the Lord Jesus.

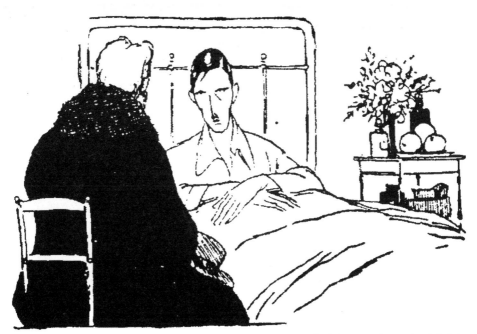

Some close church friends and the minister and elders gathered with his family around his bed and there the Scriptures were read, prayer was made to God, some words of encouragement were spoken and they all sang together the words of several hymns they greatly loved. I was told that, mixed with the sadness, there was a true joy because the one who was dying would soon be with the lover of his soul, the Lord Jesus Christ.

As we are told in today's reading, Christians have had the 'sting of death' removed. Christ died upon the cross to remove sin's punishment from all his people.

It may appear that the grave has the victory, but the day is coming when the earth will release the remains of the dead and all will rise again. God's people will rise in glory with resurrected bodies similar to that of the Lord Jesus. Non-Christians too will rise again, but they will face the judgement of Christ and be sent to everlasting punishment.

The curse of death will then be gone and heaven's inhabitants will praise God saying, 'Thanks be to God, who gives us the victory through our Lord Jesus Christ' (1 Corinthians 15:57). Then we shall know the reality of the words in our reading: 'Death is swallowed up in victory. O Death, where is your sting? O Hades [or, "grave"], where is your victory?' (1 Corinthians 15:55).

All who belong to Christ can face death with confidence because they know the reality of the words: 'I live by faith in the Son of God, who loved me and gave himself for me' (Galatians 2:20). Christians know that in their final moments on earth Christ will be with them, giving them all the encouragement and support they need. They have the assurance that they will be able to say with David of old:

Yea, though I walk through the valley of the shadow of death,
I will fear no evil; for you are with me;
Your rod and your staff, they comfort me

(Psalm 23:4).

To think about

1. What is physical death?
2. What is spiritual death?
3. What does it mean when we say that Christians have the victory over death?

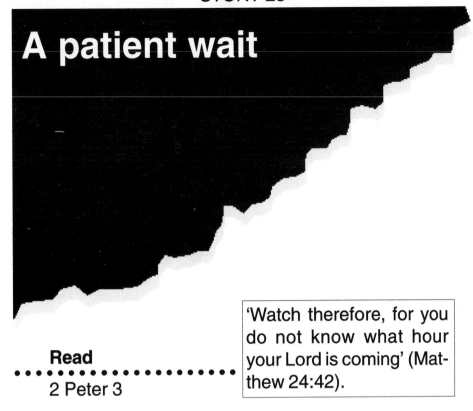

A patient wait

Read

2 Peter 3

'Watch therefore, for you do not know what hour your Lord is coming' (Matthew 24:42).

Every Christian has the expectation in his or her heart that Christ will one day return. This is one of our great 'hopes'. When you and I use the word 'hope' we mean that something may or may not come to pass, although we would rather it did happen. But in the Scriptures when we read the word 'hope' it speaks of a certainty. Writing to Titus Paul speaks of Christians who were 'looking for the blessed hope and glorious appearing of our great God and Saviour Jesus Christ' (Titus 2:13).

Paul was declaring that God's people can be sure and certain that their Saviour, Jesus Christ, will one day return to this earth. All who belong to him are called upon to wait patiently for the great day to arrive.

If you are expecting something good to happen I feel sure you say to your Mum or Dad, 'When is it going to happen? I just can't wait!'

Many years ago we were having visitors to tea. As they weren't sure where we lived I decided to drive to their home and bring them to our house. Wanting the daily paper, I asked two of our girls to come with me in the car so that they could buy the paper while I collected our visitors. Dropping the girls off at the paper shop, I told them to wait till I returned: 'I'll just collect our visitors and be back. I shouldn't be more than a couple of minutes.'

Vicki and Heather trusted their dad and happily set off to buy the paper. However, when I collected the visitors I just drove them home, forgetting about the two girls who were waiting for their 'reliable' dad to return and collect them.

After entertaining our visitors for half an hour Val said, 'Tea is ready. Call the girls, Jim.'

Then I had a horrible feeling as Cathie and Lisa came in to wash their hands ready for the evening meal. Vicki and Heather were missing and I realized that I knew where they were. Val turned to me with a look of surprise, saying, 'Oh Jim, you didn't forget them?'

I quickly jumped into the car and drove downtown to the newsagent. I felt so relieved when I saw them both standing outside the paper shop patiently waiting.

'You took a long time,' said Vicki. 'What happened?'

I stuttered out my explanation and praised them for being so obedient.

Heather then said that several people had offered to drive them home, but they had both said, 'No. Dad said he was coming and told us to wait for him.' They trusted me to return.

Every so often when the family get together I'm reminded about the time I forgot my two daughters!

Our reading speaks very plainly of the return of the Lord Jesus Christ. He who is our Saviour will return and gather his people together to be with him for ever. There are many people who laugh at our 'hope'. They tell us that we are fools to believe such a ridiculous story. However, we can trust our Lord. We are not the foolish ones. The day is coming 'when the Lord Jesus is revealed from heaven with his mighty angels, in flaming fire taking vengeance on those who do not know God, and on those who do not obey the gospel of our Lord Jesus Christ' (2 Thessalonians 1:7-8).

What a wonderful day that will be! For the first time we shall see our Lord and Saviour face to face. We shall be able to praise him perfectly because we then shall have been made perfectly righteous.

However, we must wait with joyful anticipation for that wonderful day to come. And how are we to spend our waiting days? Peter tells us that we are to live a godly life of obedience to the Lord Jesus. It may seem to be a long wait, but God is giving people time to repent of their sins. Repentance and faith in Christ will be impossible for unbelievers after Christ appears in glory.

Let us all prepare for that day when Christ again breaks into history. Let us live the life of faith, rejoicing in our salvation, patiently waiting for the appearing of our great God and Saviour, Jesus Christ.

To think about

1. How long is it since Christ spoke the words in our text?
2. Our reading came from Peter's epistle. Who was Peter and what is an epistle?
3. What is an angel? (See Hebrews 1:14; Mark 12:25; Psalm 68:17; 91:11-12).
4. Do you think you will become an angel when you reach heaven? What makes you give that answer?

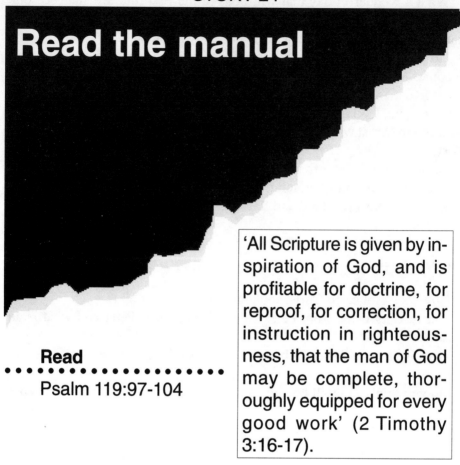

Read the manual

Read
• • • • • • • • • • • • • • • • • •
Psalm 119:97-104

'All Scripture is given by inspiration of God, and is profitable for doctrine, for reproof, for correction, for instruction in righteousness, that the man of God may be complete, thoroughly equipped for every good work' (2 Timothy 3:16-17).

The book which has the greatest sales throughout the world is the Bible. However, I wonder if it is the most read book?

We have many books on our shelves that just sit there and are rarely opened and read. I have a book on my shelf which was published over one hundred years ago. In all those years it has not been read because the pages are still stuck together. No paper knife has opened those pages.

Not long ago I had an appointment to visit the doctor. It was my monthly visit and I made the appointment a week before I needed to go. The secretary gave me a card with the date and time of my visit which I carefully put in my wallet.

When the day came, I got out of bed a little earlier than usual, and prepared myself for the visit. I was the doctor's first patient of the day — the appointment was for 8 a.m. Soon I was quietly sitting in the waiting room and I nodded to Dr King as he walked past me and into his room.

Then the secretary came over to me and smiling broadly said, 'Jim, your appointment is not today. You're here a day early. Come back tomorrow morning and the doctor will see you.'

'But,' I replied, taking the card out of my pocket, 'the card you gave me said today at 8 a.m.'

Then I went very red in the face and you can imagine why. I had carried the card about with me and hadn't bothered to check what was written on it. I thought I knew what was there.

That has happened quite frequently with me, especially when it comes to my computer. I have a heap of manuals which I haven't read. When I ask someone for help in working with a particular programme I'm asked, 'Have you read the manual?' When I reply, 'No,' I'm told to get it out and read it carefully.

Manuals are very important in giving an understanding of how machines and programmes work. Recently when listening to the radio I heard the announcer make the comment: 'The earth is the only planet that came with a manual for the inhabitants.' He was not a Christian, but was referring to the fact that the citizens of the earth had been given the Ten Commandments as a rule of life.

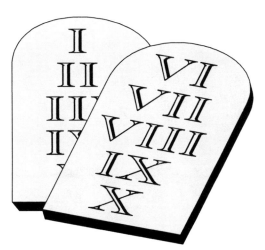

The Bible is God's manual to everyone. It is the word of the living God, explaining our sinful condition and pointing sinners to the Saviour, the Lord Jesus Christ. The Bible is God's history of salvation, telling of the wonderful way he made preparations for the coming of his Son to save sinners. The Scriptures urge sinners to believe on the Lord Jesus Christ if they wish to be saved.

As far as Christians are concerned, the Bible should be the best-read book on their bookshelf. However, the fact is that the majority of people don't bother to read the Bible. They have little or no idea of the truths contained in its pages.

Christians should be able to say with David, 'How sweet are your words to my taste, sweeter than honey to my mouth!' We must also be able to say with the psalmist, 'Oh, how I love your law!' The law of God is perfect and should be a delight to the heart and mind of everyone. Is this true of you? Are you one who reads the whole Bible — both Old and New Testaments? We should all know what God has to say to us.

May you be one of those people who read and meditate upon the Word of God. As we do this we are taught how we should live. Then in our lives we bring glory to our God and Saviour, the Lord Jesus Christ.

To think about

1. What is the Bible and how many books are contained in the Old and New Testaments?
2. Why should I believe what is written in my Bible?
3. How was it that the writers of the various books were kept from writing any errors? Read and discuss 2 Peter 1:21 and 2 Timothy 3:16.

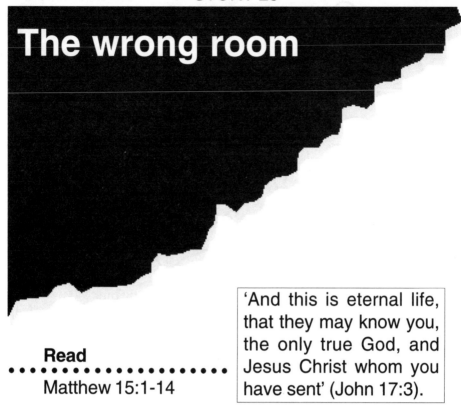

The wrong room

Read

Matthew 15:1-14

'And this is eternal life, that they may know you, the only true God, and Jesus Christ whom you have sent' (John 17:3).

Blindness is a tragedy. To live in a world of such wonderful shapes and colours and not to be able to appreciate the beauty around us is a great misfortune. Most of us have good eyesight, even if we wear spectacles, but we fail to take much notice of the world about us. How many have really looked at the bees working with the pollen, or noticed the great range of colours in the leaves on the trees? Yes, many of us have eyes, but do not see the wonder of the creation in which we live.

The same is so true of spiritual truth. Too many people believe spiritual lies because they have never bothered to search through the Scriptures to discover the truth. They just drift along.

My brother and his wife once lived in a manse beside a doctor's surgery. Many people visiting the surgery parked their cars in front of the manse or in the church parking area. This was very convenient when they had an appointment with the doctor in such a busy area of a large city.

One morning, John's wife Elizabeth decided to rest for a while. She had been working hard all morning and now it was

time to sit down with a cup of tea and take it easy for a few minutes. However, you can imagine her surprise when she entered her living room and discovered a lady sitting in her favourite chair, reading one of the magazines from the coffee table. When Elizabeth entered the room the lady, who was not looking well, asked, 'Is the doctor on time?'

You can only try to picture the look on the lady's face when Elizabeth told her she was in the lounge of a private house and not in the doctor's waiting room.

'But I thought this was the doctor's waiting room,' she stuttered. Then, with very humble apologies, the lady stood up and left the manse saying, 'I'm so sorry! I should be more careful in future. I just didn't look at the address.'

If Elizabeth had not gone into the room the lady might have waited there for hours.

And that is what is happening in so many churches. Not all pastors teach the truth, but often people just wander into the nearest church, sit down and listen to leaders who may not be teaching biblical truth.

Now a question to my readers: are you attending a biblically based church? Are you being fed good spiritual food each Lord's Day? Do you check the truth of what your pastor is teaching, using the Bible as the standard against which to test what is taught? In the book of Acts the

Berean Jews were praised because they did not accept Paul's teaching without comparing it with the teaching found in the Scriptures. They wanted to be certain that Paul was teaching God's truth: 'These were more fair-minded than those in Thessalonica, in that they received the word with all readiness, and searched the Scriptures daily to find out whether these things were so' (Acts 17:11).

Today, people from a variety of sects knock on our doors teaching lies. They are like the Pharisees of old who appeared to be very religious people, yet were blind leaders of the blind. They were leading people to hell.

You and I must not only know what we believe, but also why we believe such teachings. We must not be like that woman who was sitting in the wrong room. She thought all was well, but that was not so. In that room she wouldn't find any treatment for her illness — she needed to go into the doctor's waiting room.

We must all be aware of the fact that Satan is out there doing all he can to lead people astray. He wants to prevent them from going to Christ for salvation. He works hard to cause Christians to fall into sin, so that they bring dishonour on God. He knows he can never finally entice them away from Christ because the Lord Jesus said of all who belong to him, 'And I give them eternal life, and they shall never perish; neither shall anyone snatch them out of my hand' (John 10:28). Satan knows, however, that if a believer falls into terrible sin that person's witness will be ruined.

We are warned in Scripture about those who perform 'great signs and wonders' in an effort to deceive even God's own chosen people, 'the elect' (Matthew 24:24). This can in fact never happen, because God will not allow his own people to be led astray permanently, but we are warned to be on our guard.

So, let us all make sure we are sitting in the right church — one which honours God and teaches the truth as it is found in God's Word. We don't agree on all issues, but the church of the Lord Jesus throughout the world holds the basic truths in common. All God's people should love each other, knowing that we are all Christians, born of the Holy Spirit and saved through faith alone. We all acknowledge that Christ our Saviour is the Lord, the Second Person of the Trinity, the only mediator between God and man.

May God bless each one of us and may we all be sitting in the correct room!

To think about

1. What did Christ mean when he called the Pharisees 'blind leaders'? Read Matthew 15:14.
2. How do people become defiled, and what can be done about it?
3. The scribes and Pharisees accused the disciples of not washing their hands before eating. Why did they consider this to be a serious matter?

It's hot here!

Read
• • • • • • • • • • • • • • • • • • • •
Revelation 20:7-15

'It is a fearful thing to fall into the hands of the living God' (Hebrews 10:31).

Our text tells us a great truth in a few words: God judges the unconverted and his judgement is one of absolute terror to those who are strangers to Christ.

There is a judgement day coming, despite what the world would have us believe. The day is getting closer when we shall all stand before the judgement seat of King Jesus and there give an account of our lives.

Christians do not fear that day because the one who is the Judge is also their Saviour. We know the truth of God's Word, where it is written: 'There is therefore now no condemnation to those who are in Christ Jesus, who do not walk according to the flesh, but according to the Spirit' (Romans 8:1). We belong to Christ. Our sins have been forgiven and we are clothed in his righteousness. As Christ bore our punishment on the cross God does not punish those for whom Christ died.

However, if you are one of those who live for yourself and the things of the world, you will face the anger of an offended God. The Scriptures say of an angry God, 'Our God is a consuming fire' (Hebrews 12:29).

When I was young, many homes had no electric light. My wife grew up on a farm and in her young days electricity was not connected to the house. Her mum had to light the fire to cook a meal, there was an ice-chest in

which to store food, the clothes were ironed with an iron heated by methylated spirits — life was difficult.

When night came, out came the kerosene lamps and on some occasions the candles. The lamp never really gave enough light to make reading easy.

Another difficulty with the lamp was caused by the insects that were attracted to the naked flame. They came from everywhere and fluttered around the light. If there was a globe around the flame insects smashed themselves into the hot glass. They were attracted to the light. Sometimes the moths and other insects flew too close to the hot flame and died — burned to death.

And this is what will happen on the Day of Judgement to all who have not repented of their sins and come to Christ for salvation. They spend a lifetime playing on the brink of hell, the place of punishment. Then following judgement they will be consigned to that awful place of which we read, 'And the smoke of their torment ascends for ever and ever; and they have no rest day or night...' (Revelation 14:11). Yes, it is a 'fearful thing to fall into the hands of the living God'.

Today the majority of people fear events that might happen to them in this world. They are afraid to walk down the street because of 'muggers'. They lock their homes in an effort to prevent burglars breaking in. They fear the possibility of war, or economic problems, and so on.

The Lord Jesus had something to say to all those who fear what will happen to them in this life. He said, 'And do not fear those who kill the body but cannot kill the soul. But rather fear him who is able to destroy both soul and body in hell' (Matthew 10:28). All who are not Christians should be afraid of the God who will judge the world in righteousness through his Son, the Lord Jesus Christ.

Our reading speaks of 'the second death' — hell, 'the lake of fire and brimstone'. May all who belong to Christ rejoice in the reality that the hands of the risen Saviour hold us safe and will not let us go. The Lord Jesus is the place of security!

To think about

1. Sinners are told that they should fear God. What does this mean? Read Matthew 10:28.
2. Discuss the first and second birth (John 3:1-8).
3. Discuss this statement: 'Born once, die twice. Born twice, die once.'

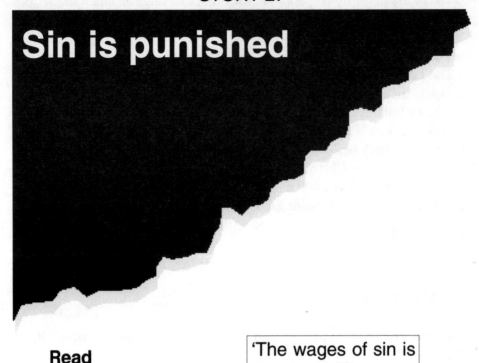

Sin is punished

Read
• • • • • • • • • • • • • • • • • • • •
2 Kings 5

'The wages of sin is death...' (Romans 6:23).

Sin pays wages and the Scriptures outline three payments that sinners receive — in this life and the life to come. The first payment is physical death. With the exception of Enoch and Elijah and those alive at the Lord's Second Coming, every single person has died or will one day die.

Secondly, there is spiritual death. Adam died spiritually the day he sinned, and every descendant of Adam — with the exception of the Lord Jesus — has a sinful nature from the moment of conception. Even Christians were at one time spiritually dead, which means that we could not choose to put our trust in the Lord Jesus Christ for our salvation. God had to act and give us spiritual life, otherwise we would have remained in our sins. This was done when the Holy Spirit came into our hearts and we were 'born again'.

Thirdly, there is the 'second death', which is eternal punishment and which was the subject of the previous chapter. All who do not repent of their sins and come to Christ for salvation will one day experience this.

Sin pays wages and sin is punished. Many unconverted people seem to go on living in their sinful ways and never receive any punishment, while Christians often appear to experience continual suffering. However, the truth is that many non-Christians do suffer for their sins even in this life.

Many people today use illegal drugs which cause grievous problems not only for the users but also for society at large. Using infected needles has meant that some of these people now have AIDS. Obedience to the law brings its own reward. Disobedience brings problems.

Living on a farm meant that when I was young we usually had a garden where there were plenty of vegetables growing. Dotted around the edge of this garden were fruit trees. So we always had good food on our table. However, we discovered that someone was getting into the garden and stealing our fruit and vegetables. So Dad painted a sign which he nailed to a post: It read:

TRESPASSERS WILL BE PROSECUTED!
ENTER AT YOUR OWN RISK

This meant that anyone entering our farm without permission was breaking the law.

Early one morning, before the sun rose, Dad was getting ready to milk the cows when he spied a person creeping across the paddock towards our vegetable patch. Thinking it was best to ring the police and let them take action, Dad turned to go inside the house.

Suddenly he heard the bull bellow and, looking, saw Ferdinand with his head down, racing towards the intruder. The man stopped still, then turned and ran for the fence. Now Ferdinand was really quick on his hooves and he was covering the ground much faster than the man. Gradually he gained on the thief, who dropped his bag as he raced for his life. Both reached the

fence at the same time. The man dived under the wire, hoping he would be safe, while the bull just kept going straight into the fence. There was a tangle of wire, hooves, legs, clothes and a mixture of screaming for help and loud bellowing. As Ferdinand had wire caught around his legs the man managed to reach his car and escaped down the road. When we arrived at the fence we found bits of clothing with blood-stains. Ferdinand wasn't very happy and Dad had to be very careful as he went about releasing him from the wire.

Some time later we discovered the name of the person who had tried to steal our vegetables. For weeks he walked with a limp and on several parts of his body he carried scars which would always remind him of the day he broke God's law by trying to steal our property. His sin caused him much trouble. I know of other people whose particular sins caused much heartache.

In the story of Naaman and God's gracious dealing with him through the prophet Elisha we see how the greed of the prophet's servant had terrible consequences. Gehazi knew that his master Elisha would not accept any gift when Naaman had been cured of his leprosy, yet he deliberately lied to Naaman in order to get some clothes and money. When Elisha asked Gehazi where he had been, he once again lied. Gehazi's lies and greed resulted in Naaman's leprosy being transferred to him. His sin was punished in a way that meant he would in future be an outcast from society. No longer would he be able to take part in the religious activities of the Jewish people. His life was in ruins.

Think of Uzzah, who touched the ark of the covenant and was struck down by God (2 Samuel 6:6-7). Uzzah knew the law of God and by disobeying the commandment of the Lord invited the wrath of the holy God whom he had offended.

In the New Testament we read of Ananias and Sapphira who were struck down because they lied to God, the Holy Spirit (Acts 5:5-11). Then there were those Corinthian Christians who came to the Lord's Supper so unprepared that God punished them with sickness, and in extreme cases death (1 Corinthians 11:30).

All sin is punished. Some may escape punishment in this life, but the Day of Judgement will be the time when justice is administered.

In Psalm 73 we find the psalmist Asaph questioning why people who lived their lives without reference to God seemed to escape punishment for their sinful ways. He saw that many unbelievers enjoyed life to the full. He even began to question whether it was worthwhile serving God, until he 'went into the sanctuary of God'. It was then he 'understood their end' because he realized that all such people would 'perish' (Psalm 73:17-18,27).

If we have true faith in Christ may this be evident in the way we live. May we all turn away from sin before it is too late and go on to live a life of obedience to Christ out of love for him.

To think about

1. Who was Naaman and what country did he come from?
2. What is leprosy?
3. From the story of Ananias and Sapphira we learn that the Holy Spirit is God. Explain how this truth is taught (Read Acts 5:3-4).

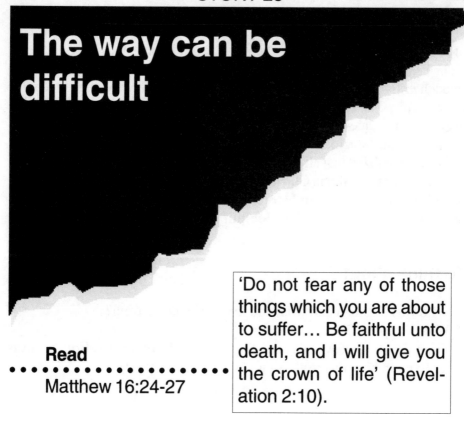

The way can be difficult

Read
• •
Matthew 16:24-27

'Do not fear any of those things which you are about to suffer... Be faithful unto death, and I will give you the crown of life' (Revelation 2:10).

If you belong to Christ then the words of today's reading apply to you. You must be ready to deny yourself daily, take up your God-given cross and then faithfully follow the Saviour. Carrying a cross was not a pleasant experience because it meant that at the end of the road the person carrying the cross would be nailed to it and left there to die a horrible death. So we see from this passage that following Christ can at times be very difficult.

Everyone has stressful times, but the Christian usually suffers more than most in this world. He not only experiences all the problems of daily life in common with other people, but he suffers because he is a Christian. It is sad to say, but the world generally does not like the Christian faith. That is why Christians are persecuted. Our text was written to the Christians at Smyrna who were about to endure great persecution simply because they loved and served Christ. But it is all worthwhile because the day is coming when Christ's people will meet him face to face and be welcomed into the kingdom he has prepared for them.

One day Val and I bought some food from McDonalds and after driving along the road for several minutes we stopped the car and ate our meal under a shady tree. Life was so pleasant. We had food to eat, the country-side looked great and all was quiet. Then we saw an amazing sight — a black crow was flying along with great difficulty. The bird was losing height

as it struggled to stay in the air and keep moving. We could see its problem. The crow had also visited McDonalds, but McDonalds' rubbish tip, where it had picked up a discarded milk-shake carton containing something it wanted. So there it was, struggling to keep airborne, wings beating as fast as possible, with the container dangling from its beak. The poor bird was making hard work of it and, the last we saw of it, it was sinking ever closer to the ground while its wings were flapping faster and faster.

Life at that time was difficult for that crow! Somehow I don't think it crash-landed or lost the food in the container. I like to think it made it to its nest where it enjoyed its meal from McDonalds.

The Christian life is sometimes like the experience of that crow. Life has its many problems. When people discover we love the Lord many turn their backs upon us and no longer call us their friends. Some Christians have lost their job because they would not cheat for their boss. In some parts of the world Christians are persecuted and killed just because they love Jesus, their Lord and Saviour. This is really taking up one's cross and following the Lord.

The Lord has made great promises to his persecuted people, one of which we find in Matthew 5:10-12: 'Blessed are those who are persecuted for righteousness' sake, for theirs is the kingdom of heaven. Blessed are you when they revile and persecute you, and say all kinds of evil against you falsely for my sake. Rejoice and be exceedingly glad, for great is your reward in heaven, for so they persecuted the prophets who were before you.'

Young people can be mocked because they attend Sunday School and worship with God's people. This cruel behaviour is very unpleasant and can be very hurtful. If this is happening to you, hold up your head and be courageous. God loves his children and will never let them down. Remember his promise that your reward in heaven will be 'great'. It is the scoffers who are the losers. We should feel sorry for them!

Keep your eyes on the Lord Jesus, who suffered so much in order that his people might be saved. He willingly sacrificed his life for his people.

Many people spend a lifetime struggling to put together as much as they can of the things of the world. The Lord Jesus has no part in their lives and so they lose their souls. Christians, fight on, be courageous, live as Christ would have you live and seek always to do all things in a way which will bring praise and honour to God. The struggle is worthwhile. Never give up!

To think about

1. In what way have you been forced to suffer for the sake of the Lord Jesus?
2. How should Christians react when they are persecuted for Christ's sake?
3. Read the story of someone who made great sacrifices for his Saviour — e.g. John G. Paton, David Brainerd, Martin Luther, John Newton, Bill Borden of Yale.

Our God is faithful — he never leaves his people!

Read
• •
Acts 7:54-60

'For he himself has said, "I will never leave you nor forsake you"' (Hebrews 13:5).

The writer of the epistle to the Hebrews was instructing the Hebrew Christians to live a godly life. This must have been hard to accept as they were surrounded by people who hated them and their faith. The worldly people seemed to be prospering and had so many of the world's good things that the Christians began to question whether following Christ was really worthwhile. However, the writer told them to be content with the things they already had. They were not to covet the possessions of other people because they had the most precious possession of all — they had Christ with them and God was overshadowing them with his amazing love.

He then reminded them all of God's promise to his people that he would never leave them — no, he would never forsake them. This was not a new promise from God, as he had said the same to Joshua when he was about to lead the Israelites into the promised land (Joshua 1:5).

These are encouraging words which we should believe with all our hearts. In the original language in which it was written, the text says something like this: 'I will never, no, never leave you, nor ever forsake you.' The words stress the truth that God will never abandon his people, no matter what the circumstances.

Some time ago there was a sea accident off the coast of Australia. A submarine had surfaced for some running repairs. The captain sent men out

109

onto the hull to do what was necessary before the submarine could continue on its underwater journey. When the work was complete the captain gave word for the men to climb back through the conning tower to safety. Somehow two young sailors did not hear the command and they worked on. Imagine their horror when they heard the engines start up and the submarine begin to move forward and then submerge.

It was some hours before the captain realized that all the men had not returned from their work duty. Quickly the submarine surfaced, turned around and, with sailors keeping watch, made its way back to the spot at which it had dived. Sad to say, the bodies of the two young sailors were never found — they had drowned at sea. Since that tragedy, submarine captains are required to carry out a very careful check of all the men when work is done at sea, making sure that every sailor is safely back on board before the instruction is given to submerge.

The Scriptures tell us that God never leaves his people, no matter what. All who belong to Christ will never perish eternally. In all the circumstances of life Christ is with us by his Spirit.

Our God is perfectly good, wise, all-powerful, faithful and holy. No one can prevent him from watching over and caring for his people. There may be times when we feel that God is far away from us, but that is not so! We should forget our feelings and trust in the word of our God who has said, 'I will never leave you nor forsake you.'

If God is always with us and never forsakes us, we can then say with the writer to the Hebrews, 'The LORD is my helper; I will not fear. What can man do to me?' (Hebrews 13:6).

When Stephen was being stoned to death he not only sensed the presence of God with him, but his spiritual eyes were opened and he 'saw the glory of God, and Jesus standing at the right hand of God' (Acts 7:55).

People will do their worst, but Christ will be with his people. God is 'a very present help in trouble' (Psalm 46:1). In Psalm 23:4 David wrote words that every believer can say with confidence:

Yea, though I walk through the valley of the shadow of death,
I will fear no evil; for you are with me;
Your rod and your staff they comfort me.

We must believe the words and promises of our God. Then we can face the future with confidence.

To think about

1. If God has promised that he will never forsake his people, why do Christians suffer in this world? Read Romans 8:28; Deuteronomy 8:5; Hebrews 12:6.
2. Who was Stephen?
3. Why are the words of Psalm 23:4 so precious to Christians?

No more fighting please!

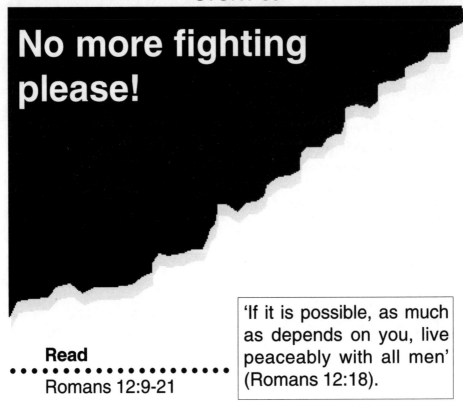

Read
• • • • • • • • • • • • • • • • • • • •
Romans 12:9-21

'If it is possible, as much as depends on you, live peaceably with all men' (Romans 12:18).

There are many occasions when parents say to their children, 'Stop that arguing. Settle down and be quiet. Show a bit of kindness to one another when you play!' I know my mum used to say that to John and me, and Val and I said it to our girls at various times when tempers frayed or play became a bit too wild.

The Lord expects his people to live at peace with one another. Of course the world wants to hurt Christians and the church, and there are times when we must put up with cruelty on the part of the unbelieving people around us. However, we must make every effort to live at peace with everyone. Our

God is the God of peace who established peace between himself and his sinful people through the saving life and death of his Son, the Lord Jesus Christ.

Jesus said, 'Blessed are the peacemakers, for they shall be called sons of God' (Matthew 5:9). It is best to avoid arguments that break friendships. There are some people who are difficult to get along with, but we are to live peacefully with them — 'as much as depends on' us.

There are times when it is not possible to live peacefully with someone else even when we have made every effort God requires of us (Hebrews 12:14). Always remember that in our efforts to establish friendships we must never sacrifice the truth.

Some time ago we had to 'babysit' a cat. Now we have nothing against cats — in fact Val likes the little furry animals. However, we soon found out that there was a family member who hated that cat. When Wags, our dog, saw it walk into his house he flew at it, barking loudly and with teeth bared. The cat knew war was about to break out, so up went its fur and tail and out went its paw, slapping Wags on the face. He backed off, still barking, unsure of what he should do next. And that's how it went on for the next week. Wags would bark and the cat would hit out at him. Sometimes he sneaked up behind the cat and nipped it on the tail, but he was quick to make his escape as he knew that the claws hurt.

One day we noticed that when the cat first came inside in the morning it rubbed against Wags. Then a day later we saw them both eating from the same dish. They were beginning to live together peacefully. A couple of weeks later they started playing with one another. Wags chased the cat, which jumped up on the armchair. Then Wags jumped up on the chair after it. When the paw slapped Wags we could see that the claws were not protruding. The warfare was all in fun. The worst of enemies had become friends.

The cat has now returned to its owner and when Wags visits they rub against each other, chase one another around the garden and really enjoy one another's company.

Now we are to live in peace and harmony with one another. This may mean that we have to make a lot of effort to overcome difficulties, but God requires that of his people. Remember our text: '… as much as depends on you, live peaceably with all men.'

Today we find that men and women who were involved on opposite sides in the fighting of World War II are willing to shake hands and become friends. They may never forget what happened, but they are able to forgive.

Let us remember the words of the Lord Jesus: 'A new commandment I give to you, that you love one another; as I have loved you, that you also love one another. By this all will know that you are my disciples, if you have love for one another' (John 13:34-35).

When peace cannot be established make sure you are not to blame. Always show Christian love to the other person because in that way you may win his friendship. Remember the advice of the apostle Paul:

Therefore
'If your enemy is hungry, feed him;
If he is thirsty, give him a drink;
For in so doing you will heap coals of fire on his head'
                  (Romans 12:20, quoting Proverbs 25:21-22).

To think about

1. How are you to treat those people who are not friendly towards you?
2. What is meant by Christian love? Read the story of the Good Samaritan (Luke 10:25-37).
3. How do you show other members of your family that you love them?

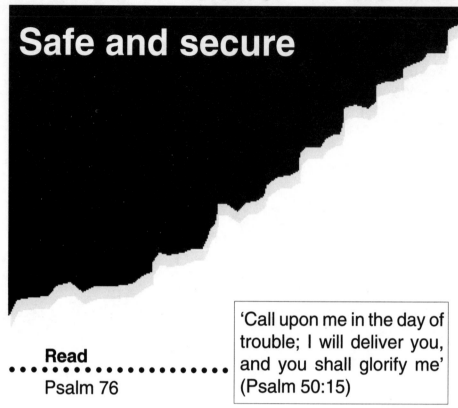

Safe and secure

Read
• • • • • • • • • • • • • • • • • • • •
Psalm 76

'Call upon me in the day of trouble; I will deliver you, and you shall glorify me' (Psalm 50:15)

Psalm 76 describes the glory and power of God as he pronounces judgement upon an ungodly world. The message of the psalm is that unrepentant sinners should fear God. The day is coming when all who have not repented and trusted in Christ will be punished for their sins. Such people should truly fear God because their future is too horrible to contemplate. However, there is a place of security which is to be found in the Lord Jesus Christ.

My little Wags is frightened by noise, especially sudden loud noise. When there is a storm and the thunder begins to rumble in the distance he creeps

close to Val or me. When the noise gets very loud he jumps up on the settee and pushes himself onto Val's lap. He looks around, shivering fearfully each time there is a clap of thunder. Wags is very sensible as he knows that there is a place of safety when the thunder starts.

One night, when Val had gone to bed, I was quietly reading in the lounge. All was very peaceful when I decided to put my feet up on a small metal table I had in front of my chair. As I did so the table suddenly collapsed with a great bang.

Poor Wags jumped to his feet. He had been sound asleep, without a care in the world. However, now his world had been turned upside down. There was a loud noise and when he saw the table he knew things were not as they should be. I could see the fear in his eyes as he took off for our bedroom where he knew Val was in bed, reading.

Normally, if Wags wants to jump up on the bed, he stands at the foot of the bed and then carefully jumps. However, this time he just ran and took a great leap. He made it onto the bed in one bound and then snuggled down next to Val. His nose disappeared under her arm and there he lay shivering in fear. Our Wags is not always a brave dog, but he is not stupid. He knows where there is safety — somewhere near Val or me.

There are times when we all need a place of security. When young people are hurt they find some security by getting close to someone they love. In Israel of old when the land of Canaan was being divided God established 'cities of refuge' for people who accidentally killed another person. As long as they remained in one of those special cities they were secure from those who wanted to avenge the death of the person killed (Numbers 35:25-28).

Now God has provided a place of security for his people, and that place of security is Jesus Christ, who has invited to himself all who feel the weight of their sins: 'Come to me, all you who labour and are heavy laden, and I

will give you rest. Take my yoke upon you and learn from me, for I am gentle and lowly in heart, and you will find rest for your souls' (Matthew 11:28-29). Those who hide in Christ will never experience the anger of God.

All who have found salvation in Christ love God and are devoted to the Lord Jesus. They hold God in awe and wonder that he, who is holy and righteous in all his ways, should bother about sinful people. How we should thank God for giving us such a wonderful Saviour! Let us fear God with a holy fear. Let it never be said of any who read these words that you were not willing to turn to Christ and be saved.

To Christ sinners must go, for salvation is to be freely found in him. As soon as you become conscious of your sins go at once to him, asking him to become your Saviour. Don't trust yourself to your good works or church attendance. These things are good, but cannot save anyone. Jesus Christ alone can save sinners.

To think about

1. Why is God angry with sinners?
2. Who is Jesus Christ, and why is he a place of safety from God's anger?
3. Why should Christians love God?
4. Try to find the names of the 'cities of refuge' (See Joshua 20).

A golden chain

'… being confident of this very thing, that he who has begun a good work in you will complete it until the day of Jesus Christ' (Philippians 1:6).

Read
• • • • • • • • • • • • • • • • • •
Romans 8:28-39

There are too many professing Christians who still have doubts about their salvation. They say they have trusted their salvation to the Lord Jesus. In their daily life others can see the fruit of the Spirit. They love God and other people and make real sacrifices to follow Christ. However, on occasions they have doubts whether their sins have all been forgiven. They wonder if they will reach heaven. It could be that sometimes you are such a person. Always remember that your doubts mean that you are not totally trusting in the promises of God in Christ.

Today's text says very plainly that if God has begun that wonderful work of salvation in your heart, he will keep that work going until you finally stand before the throne of Christ with that great number of people, and there sing his praises and enjoy the new creation for ever.

The Bible reading, especially the words found in verses 28-30, should bring comfort to your troubled heart. Trust God who made that great promise

119

because he who called you to faith in Christ will glorify you, to the praise and honour of his glorious grace. Our God will never let us down!

In these few verses we find a series of words that are linked together — foreknowledge, predestination, calling, justification and glorification. These words go together like the links of a chain. Some writers have called them 'the golden chain'.

Now chains are very important in your life and mine. In my car engine there is a chain. In Val's washing machine there is a chain. If you have a bike it will have a chain. Not far from where I live there is a sawmill where chains are widely used. When a chain breaks machinery comes to a stop.

Some time ago I was driving along a roadway which was used by many huge timber trucks, which carry very large logs to the sawmill to be cut up. The trucks usually move along at a fast pace and it is dangerous to overtake

them. I was just content to drive along thirty or forty metres behind the log truck. I didn't want to get too close as stones were being thrown up by its tyres. I also had the feeling that the logs could fall off the truck.

I knew that when the logs were loaded the men chained them into place. The chains were pulled very tight with a lever and usually were safe and secure. However, chains are only as good as the weakest link.

Without warning one chain burst apart and the back section of the logs fell off the truck and were dragged along the road. No one was hurt, but the road was blocked for some hours while a crane returned the logs to the truck.

Chains can break and it was only a couple of weeks after that incident when a lady was killed by another broken chain. The chain holding the logs in place snapped and while the logs remained safely in place on that occasion the big metal link bounced on the roadway and through the front window of the car behind. The lady who was driving that car was struck by the link and killed. It is true — metal chains do break on occasions!

But God's golden chain of salvation can never break. All those upon whom God has set his love — those 'he foreknew' — will certainly be saved and one day glorified in the presence of the Lord Jesus.

If God has set his love upon you, it means that he has predestined you to eternal life. This means the day will come when the Holy Spirit visits your life and so changes you that you have a new heart which loves God and desires to serve and worship the Lord Jesus. Your life will be so changed that you will want to be obedient to the commands of the Saviour. It also means that in the court of heaven you will be justified — forgiven and declared righteous in God's sight. The final step in God's 'golden chain' of salvation is glorification. This means we shall be given new glorified bodies like that of the Saviour and shall experience the reality of seeing Christ face to face and of having a home in the new creation that God has prepared for his people. There you, with all of God's people, will praise and magnify God and his Son who loved you and gave himself for you.

In the chapters which follow we shall have a look at the links that make up God's 'golden chain' of salvation.

To think about

1. Why is the 'chain' described as a '*golden* chain'?
2. Give two reasons why God's promises come to pass.
3. Who are the people who glorify and praise God? Why do they do this?

For my good

'And we know that all things work together for good to those who love God, to those who are the called according to his purpose' (Romans 8:28).

Read
• • • • • • • • • • • • • • • • • • • •
Hebrews 12:1-11

Many things happen to each one of us and we sometimes ask the question: 'Why is this happening to me? What is God's purpose in what he is doing?'

I have asked the question many times. Sometimes I think I have come to understand the reason why God brought certain things to pass in my life. However, at the time when the event was happening I couldn't understand why.

When the first Cromarty settlers from Scotland arrived in Australia they were given a large grant of land in a most beautiful part of the world — Port Stephens. Captain William Cromarty received 420 acres of land along the shores of one of the most picturesque harbours in the world. Two large headlands dominate the entrance to the very large harbour. The grant of land stretched along the harbour foreshores overlooking the wide stretch of clear blue water that went on and on for miles. But do we own and enjoy that land today? No!

122

Soon after the turn of the twentieth century the Australian Government decided to take back the land for use as a naval base. My ancestors fought through the courts to prevent this happening, but the land was forcibly taken by an act of parliament. The government paid several thousand pounds in compensation for the land they took back, but never used it for a naval base. Later the land was sold to private citizens and the local council for many millions of dollars.

John and I once sat down and talked about what it might have been like for us if we still had possession of that land. Yes, I think we would have been millionaires and wasting our lives in worldly pleasure. I'm sure my ancestors wondered why their land was being taken forcibly from them. They were Christian people and probably questioned God's purpose in what was happening. John and I think we know the reason behind those events. God knows what the human heart is like and how people love money and power. Had that money come our way we would probably have had no interest in Christ and eternal life. Our interests would have been centred on money and the good life. Maybe God removed that valuable family possession for the spiritual good of many of the Cromartys.

I injured my back and was forced to retire from the ministry. At first I asked myself, 'Why has God allowed this to happen?' Could it be that I was to be given time to write books that would be a spiritual blessing to other people? If I was still in the ministry I know I would not have had time to do much writing.

123

What about Joni Eareckson Tada? Without that tragic accident, in which she broke her neck and was permanently paralysed, she may never have had the opportunity to be such a great witness to the saving grace of God in Christ.

In the Scriptures we read Christ's words: 'My grace is sufficient for you, for my strength is made perfect in weakness' (2 Corinthians 12:9). It is so true that, as Paul wrote in our text, 'All things work together for good to those who love God, to those who are the called according to his purpose.'

Think for a moment of the saving work of the Lord Jesus Christ. He suffered a hell of which we have no real understanding. Then meditate upon the glorious result of his humiliation — his people have been saved.

Our reading indicates that God chastens, or disciplines, those whom he loves because his great purpose for his people is their holiness. He wants us to be like Christ, and when life is easy there is a tendency to forget God. However, in the difficult days we turn again to our God. We pray, read our Bibles and trust ourselves to him more than ever. The hard days are our growing days.

In the events of life try to see the hand of God who is working out his purposes through you and in you. When the going gets hard make sure that you come out of that experience a better Christian than before.

May God be pleased to bless each one of us with a confidence in Paul's words: 'And we know that all things work together for good to those who love God, to those who are the called according to his purpose.'

To think about

1. Why do parents chasten their children?
2. Why does God chasten his people? (See Hebrews 12:10-11).
3. Why does our reading call sin a snare? (See Hebrews 12:1).

Loved before time began

Read
• •
Romans 9:6-24

> 'God is love'
> (1 John 4:8).

On my bookshelf I have a book with the title, *Election — Love before Time*. The author, Kenneth Johns, speaks of God's great love in choosing a people to be saved. That choice was made in eternity, before you and I were born.

In my Bible I read that God chose a people in Christ who would be saved. And when was this choice made? 'Before the foundation of the world' (Ephesians 1:4). The word 'foreknew', which we read in Romans 8:29, means more than just knowing that something is going to happen. I'm sure we all agree that God knows everything that will take place in the history of this world. But God's 'foreknowledge' involves 'forelove'. This means that in eternity God set his love upon a people whom he would present to his Son (John 6:37). This involves choice and it involves a personal relationship starting in eternity.

To put this great truth in human terms is very difficult because we cannot control the future and we only deal with the things of time and space.

Recently a young couple we know were married. Soon after their marriage they began to plan for a family. They wanted to have a baby and began preparing a room for the newcomer who was not even expected at that time. However, they talked about the 'yet-to-be infant' as if they already held him in their arms.

Soon a baby was on the way. Being modern parents they found out in advance that their child would be a girl. Dad had hoped for a boy with whom he could play cricket, but he and his wife were both delighted that soon they would have their first child. The nursery was painted pink and people began giving gifts for the expected child. Even before the baby was born they loved her very much.

The baby eventually arrived and all was well. Soon she was home where the parents proudly showed off their new daughter. And their love for her continued despite the dirty nappies, the disturbed nights, the midnight feeding of the little one and all the work that goes into caring for a new baby. Their experience helps us a little to understand what it means when we say that God set his love upon a people not yet born.

God set no conditions for his love. He did not choose people who were good and obedient, but in many cases people who were the worst of sinners. However, he also determined to change them and make them holy, obedient people who would try to love him with all their heart and mind.

The passage we have read today is difficult for most people to understand because it speaks of a God who loved Jacob and hated Esau. It speaks of God setting his love upon Abraham and then Isaac. God's electing love was not set upon Ishmael, nor was it set upon Esau.

God hardened the heart of Pharaoh, who treated the Israelites shamefully and refused to allow them to leave Egypt.

Paul knew that people who read his words would say, 'God is unfair to choose one person and leave others in their sins! Why should God love one person and hate another?' So Paul wrote an answer to their objections: 'What shall we say then? Is there unrighteousness with God? Certainly not! For he says to Moses, "I will have mercy on whomever I will have mercy, and I will have compassion on whomever I will have compassion." So then it is not of him who wills, nor of him who runs, but of God who shows mercy' (Romans 9:14-16).

Paul's use of the word 'foreknew' speaks of God's action in choosing a people to redeem. He said the same of Israel of old: 'Hear this word that the LORD has spoken against you, O children of Israel, against the whole family which I brought up from the land of Egypt, saying: "You only have I known of all the families of the earth"' (Amos 3:1,2). The God who knows everything 'knew' Israel in a saving way.

Foreknowledge, then, is the first link in God's golden chain of salvation — his action in setting his love upon a people as yet unborn. This eternal love was unconditional. We have a gracious God.

To think about

1. Why did God choose Israel as his own special people?
2. Why should God choose you for salvation?
3. God 'foreloved' his people. What does this mean?

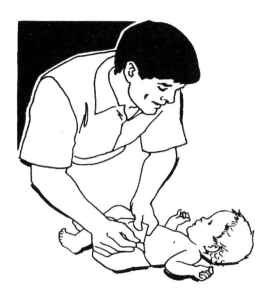

My plan didn't work out!

> 'In him also we have obtained an inheritance, being predestined according to the purpose of him who works all things according to the counsel of his will, that we who first trusted in Christ should be to the praise of his glory' (Ephesians 1:11-12).

Read
• • • • • • • • • • • • • • • • • •
Isaiah 46

Having foreknown a people, God had to translate his love into action. He had to determine beforehand the destiny of those he 'foreloved'. Nothing could be left to 'chance' and as God had determined that those he loved should be 'conformed to the image of his Son' (Romans 8:29) he took action to ensure they would become increasingly like Christ in their lives.

Now you and I make our plans, but we can never be sure they will actually be carried out. We don't have the power to make things happen exactly as we would like them to.

Many years ago I decided I wanted to become a lecturer at a teachers' training college. Several of my friends were already lecturers and I made up my mind that I would like to join them. So I settled down to some extra university study. When I had the necessary qualifications I watched the

newspapers for a job vacancy. Then one day a college position for a person with my qualifications was advertised. I applied at once thinking my plan was being fulfilled.

Before long the day arrived for my interview. Although I had made every preparation I thought was necessary, I had no control over what took place in the interview. Three men were there to question me for over an hour and I soon knew the meeting was not going as I had planned.

At last the men thanked me for coming along and told me that I would be advised of the outcome of the interview after they had met with other people who had also applied for the job. As I drove to pick up Val I felt very disappointed about the way things had gone.

I eventually parked near the police station where we had arranged to meet. It was late afternoon and the police were coming and going all the time. Then one policeman on a motorcycle pulled over beside my car and asked me to get out. When I did he ordered me to follow him and stand behind my car. As I did so he asked, 'Do you own this car?'

'Yes, sir,' I replied very politely. I didn't want to upset a policeman as I was disappointed enough with the events of that day.

'Read me your number-plate!' he demanded.

129

I read the number-plate to him and then came his reply: 'I can't see that. Your tow-bar and ball have obscured part of the letter 'J'. I can't tell if it is an 'I' or a 'J'.'

I started to stammer out that where I lived everyone had a tow-bar and ball on the car as most people were prepared at any time to tow their boats to the river for a day on the water. No one troubled to remove the tow-ball. However, he wasn't impressed with my excuse and I received a fine.

You see what was happening to me. My plan to become a lecturer at teachers' college had come to nothing and now something I hadn't planned at all was spoiling the rest of my day. I didn't have control of my life.

The Bible tells me that if I was left to myself I would never turn to Christ for salvation. The Scriptures tell us, 'There is none righteous, no, not one … there is none who seeks after God… There is none who does good, no, not one' (Romans 3:10-12). Left to myself I would go to hell.

But God, having set his love upon a people, planned every detail of their lives. They would be made to see their sin and need of a Saviour. Then they would trust themselves to the Lord Jesus. Why would this happen? Because God made a plan in which the Holy Spirit had a part to play. These people would be 'born again' and be given saving faith. He also predetermined that they would become more and more like Christ in their life and character.

Even the good works we do have also been predetermined. Paul wrote, 'For we are his workmanship, created in Christ Jesus for good works, which God prepared beforehand that we should walk in them' (Ephesians 2:10).

I am free to make my decisions in life, yet all is predetermined. I don't understand how this can be, but this truth is taught in the Scriptures. Think of the day those wicked people killed the Lord Jesus. Peter said of that day and those people who crucified Christ, 'Him [Christ], being delivered by the determined purpose and foreknowledge of God, you have taken by lawless hands, have crucified, and put to death' (Acts 2:23). Those men who crucified Christ were totally to blame for what they did. Even though God predetermined what would happen, those who put Christ to death can never point the finger at God and say, 'You made me do it!' This whole matter is a great mystery, but it is truth. We must always remember the words of Scripture which state, 'Let no one say when he is tempted, "I am tempted by God"; for God cannot be tempted by evil, nor does he himself tempt anyone' (James 1:13). God is not the author of sin!

So we have now seen that God loved his people before time began, pre-determining how they would be saved and how they would live. It is so true that salvation is all of God.

To think about

1. What does the word 'predestination' mean? (The *Westminster Confession of Faith* puts it like this: 'God from all eternity did, by the most wise and holy counsel of his own will, freely and unchangeably ordain whatsoever comes to pass: yet so, as thereby neither is God the author of sin, nor is violence offered to the will of the creatures, nor is the liberty or contingency of second causes taken away, but rather established' — Chapter 3, Section 1).
2. How is it that God can bring to pass all his plans?
3. Why do so many of our plans come to nothing?

Can you hear what I can't?

Read
• • • • • • • • • • • • • • • • • • •
Isaiah 55:6-11

'Moreover whom he predestined, these he also called; whom he called, these he also justified; and whom he justified, these he also glorified' (Romans 8:30).

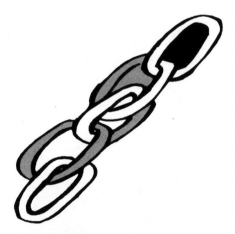

There are many different sounds to be heard each day. We live in a small, quiet village where there is not much noise. Sitting outside I can hear birds singing, dogs barking, wind rustling the leaves of the tree, children playing and a lawnmower in the distance. At the moment there is no sound of cars — in fact it is a quiet day and most days are like this.

When Val and I are inside we don't hear many of the outside noises. However, Wags is very different from me, hearing sounds I never hear. Sometimes Val and I are quietly talking, unaware of any sound outside, when Wags jumps to his feet, starts barking and runs for the door and then outside. When we have a look we usually find a person walking through the park beside our home, or a dog sniffing his way along the path. Sometimes I call Wags and he ignores me, but if I rattle the car keys he comes like a rocket thinking he might have a ride in the car.

Many times our family visited the beach. We all enjoyed surfing, shooting the waves and the happy times we had together. However, the beach is not always safe. In Australia we have to keep a watch out for the currents which can drag a swimmer out to sea. The lifesavers always put out flags indicating where it is safe to surf. These areas are usually free from dangerous currents. A second danger is sharks. Occasionally we read of a person being taken by a shark and most sensible people keep one eye on the waves and the other on the lookout for a shark-fin.

On one occasion while we were swimming someone saw a shark cruising several hundred yards out to sea and called out, 'Shark!' However, most people just went on swimming. It was a lovely day and while people heard the shouted warning, there was no real authority behind those words. Our family looked around, but kept on swimming.

Then came the sound of the siren from the beach. The ever-watchful lifesavers had seen the shark and had pressed the alarm button. It was then that most people struggled through the water to reach the safety of the sand. What surprised me was that even with the lifeguards' warning some people still continued to swim. They were unconcerned with the danger that wasn't very far away.

In our last chapter we read of God who predestined all that happens and then works to bring about those events. Having set his love upon a people and having predestined them to eternal life, God must bring his plan to fruition. In our golden chain of salvation we now come to the link named 'calling'. God calls the people upon whom he has set his love to faith in Christ. He may use the minister who preaches the gospel, a friend's witness, the giving of a tract, the reading of the Bible, or one of the many events that happen each day.

For a moment let us think of a worship service where the congregation consists of Christians and others who happen to be present. The pastor preaches a powerful sermon where people are told of their sins and need of a Saviour. God is praised in song and prayer, the Scriptures are read and people are given the opportunity of giving towards the work of the church. The Christians return to their home praising God for his goodness while the majority of the others go home and have their lunch before they go off to do their own things. However, something has happened to several non-Christians who were present. They are troubled about their sins and that is something that has not happened before. Some are weeping over their rebellion against God's holy law and now want the Lord Jesus as their Saviour.

Why the difference?

First, there is the 'external' call to repentance and faith in Christ. The pastor calls on all his hearers to repent of their sins. His words enter their ears, but for many people that is as far as they go. Why, then, do some respond to the preacher's call? The answer is that there is also an 'internal' or 'effective' call. The reason why it is 'effective' is because the Holy Spirit takes the speaker's words and drives them home to the sinner's heart. The Holy Spirit brings about a change in the person's heart so he, or she, is convicted, or made aware, of his sins and turns to the Lord Jesus Christ.

The Holy Spirit, who is God, makes it possible for those who have been 'foreknown' and 'predestined' to believe the truth and love the Lord Jesus. He makes it certain that his people hear and believe the truth.

God said through the prophet Isaiah,

So shall my word be that goes forth from my mouth;
It shall not return to me void,
But it shall accomplish what I please,
And it shall prosper in the thing for which I sent it

(Isaiah 55:11).

The fact that God has a people who are to be saved encourages all Christians to witness to the saving work of Christ. If you are a Christian, one day you will witness to someone whom God has predestined to eternal life. He will be using you to bring the good news to that person in a way which will

lead to his or her salvation. What a great privilege this is for sinful people —
to be God's instruments in taking the gospel to one of those whom God has
chosen to save!

If you are a Christian praise God for giving you hearing ears — ears that
enabled you to respond to the gracious words of salvation in Christ.

To think about

1. If you are a Christian, how did God call you to faith in Christ?
2. Read the story of Spurgeon's conversion, where you will find that God
does not always use the great and mighty to take the gospel to lost sinners.
(This can be found in *The Young Spurgeon,* by Peter Jeffery, Evangelical
Press 1992, pp.39-43, or in *Are You Really Born Again?*, by K. Philpott,
Evangelical Press, 1998, pp.137-9.)
3. If you have a Bible dictionary or a confession of faith, find out what is
meant by the word 'regeneration'.

Justified

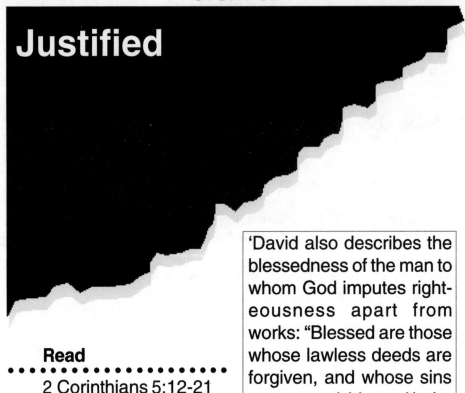

Read
• • • • • • • • • • • • • • • • • •
2 Corinthians 5:12-21

'David also describes the blessedness of the man to whom God imputes righteousness apart from works: "Blessed are those whose lawless deeds are forgiven, and whose sins are covered; blessed is the man to whom the LORD shall not impute sin"' (Romans 4:6-8).

We come now to the link in God's golden chain of salvation called 'justification'. The *Shorter Catechism* defines justification as 'an act of God's free grace, wherein he pardons all our sins, and accepts us as righteous in his sight, only for the righteousness of Christ imputed to us, and received by faith alone' (Question 33). The word 'imputes' simply means that God freely gives Christ's righteousness to his people — the righteousness of Christ is credited to our account, which is bankrupt.

Every now and again we hear of a judge who pardons a criminal. Recently I read about a man who had been found guilty of trying to smuggle drugs out of an Asian country. He was sentenced to a lifetime in jail. Now I

believe he deserved his punishment because drugs have caused so much hurt to people, to families and to nations. At the same time I know that his punishment was dreadful because of the appalling conditions in the prison in which he was to spend the remainder of his life.

Then came the king's birthday and as an act of kindness many prisoners received a royal pardon. The criminal I had been reading about was released from jail and allowed to return to his homeland. He had been pardoned and forgiven. This didn't mean he was an innocent person, just that he no longer had to pay the penalty for his crime.

When the pardon documents were presented to the officer in charge of the prison the criminals were set free. They were now liberated — not because of anything they had done, but because of the kindness of someone else — the king.

Occasionally Wags does something destructive — especially when we go out and leave him alone at home. On one occasion he found Val's spectacles and in his doggy temper he chewed the lug off the frame because he had missed out on a ride in the car. On another occasion he tore a little pillow apart. I'm sure he had great fun doing that. When we arrived home he wouldn't come out from under the settee. He was either sulking or knew he had done wrong.

We decided to keep an eye on Wags and when we found him misbehaving we gave him a smack. After he was punished we soon found that his behaviour was changing. No longer was he involved in tearing clothing. I didn't like having to smack our dear little pet and often felt like saying, 'Here, smack me instead of poor little Wags! Let him go free.' If I had done that I would have been taking the punishment for Wags' behaviour.

Justification is something that happens in the court of heaven. There, before God, the guilty sinner is declared to be forgiven and no longer under sentence of eternal death. This is possible because the Lord Jesus suffered in the guilty sinner's place. The sinner is united to the Son of God! God then looks upon the sinner through his Son. Jesus lived a life of obedience to God and he did this as the representative of his people. The righteousness of Christ is treated as belonging to his people, so God declares them to be legally righteous in his sight.

This is a wonderful transaction — my sins were placed upon Christ, and his righteousness was given to me. And how are all these blessings ours? They are ours through our God-given faith in the Lord Jesus. Faith is our link to Christ and the means by which we receive blessings upon blessings.

In this work of justification we play no part. God justifies the sinner in the court of heaven. Thus justification is a legal act of God. The Scriptures tell us 'There is none righteous, no, not one…' (Romans 3:10), but God's action in Christ imputes, or credits, righteousness to his people.

Our text tells us that God forgives the sins of his people — he covers their sins so they can be seen no more. Today's reading gives us the same truth as well as saying very plainly that those whom God 'foreknew' have 'become the righteousness of God in him [Christ]' (2 Corinthians 5:21).

We can praise God for this wonderful link in the golden chain of salvation. All God's people can rejoice as they say of Christ that he is 'The LORD our righteousness!' (Jeremiah 23:6).

To think about

1. Learn the *Shorter Catechism's* definition of justification.
2. Now explain what is meant by the biblical term 'justification'.
3. What part do you play when God justifies you? Explain what you mean by this answer.

The best is yet to be!

Read
. . . .
Revelation 21:1-8

> They shall see his face, and his name shall be on their foreheads' (Revelation 22:4).

We come now to the last link in God's golden chain of salvation. Because God has forged each of the links in his chain they cannot be broken. God set his love upon those people who were given to the Lord Jesus and the final step in God's activity is to bring them to himself in heaven. This means that the day is coming when redeemed sinners will stand in the presence of God's only Son and praise him for ever while they enjoy the wonder of the new heavens and the new earth.

God planned for all the redeemed sinners to be 'conformed to the image of his Son' (Romans 8:29). This means that all who are justified should become like Christ in all that they do, say and think.

In story 34 I told you about a young couple who had a baby girl. They loved that little girl despite the soiled nappies, the sleepless nights and all the extra work. They know they have a lot of work before them training the little one to grow up to be like them. The baby will be toilet-trained, taught

to talk, shown how to wash and dress herself and to eat with a knife and fork, as well as how to become a good citizen. The parents will pray for their little girl and teach her the ways of the Lord. They want their child to be a Christian citizen of Australia.

Many years ago I commenced my teaching career at a small school many hundreds of miles from home. It was just a small, one-teacher school well out in the bush. I enjoyed my time there, but had a longing to be home. Why? Because the girl I intended to marry lived not far from home and I wanted to be with her. We only saw one another during school holidays and our relationship was kept up by mail.

The time approached for our wedding and I could not be involved in the preparations because I lived so far away. However, Val and her parents made all the arrangements while I waited, and waited, for the time to come when I could go home. My days were spent thinking about that day when we were to be married. I purchased a new suit and new black shoes. I also booked a flat for our honeymoon.

Val and I had known each other for almost five years and December 1958 was to be so important to us. We enjoyed those five years, but each day we both could say, 'The best is yet to be!'

When the day at last arrived for me to go home, Val made preparations to meet me at the railway station.

Finally came the day when we were married. Each dressed in our best clothes, we made our vows and after the usual wedding breakfast we left for a four weeks' holiday.

There were many steps in our life leading up to that wonderful day. In some respects the events of those five years moved onwards to that important day in both our lives. Each was a link in the chain that ended in our marriage.

Christian friends, the day is coming when we shall be glorified. We shall be welcomed home by Christ when he comes again to gather us to himself.

Paul told us that God will have his people to be like Christ. This means they will become godly in all aspects of their lives. They will obey the commands of the Lord. If they disobey, God may well chastise them, just as you were chastised, or disciplined, by someone at home when you stepped out of line. The writer to the Hebrews says, 'For whom the LORD loves he chastens, and scourges every son whom he receives.' Why does he do this? Chastening is for our good, 'that we may be partakers of his holiness' (Hebrews 12:6,10). When we reach heaven and are glorified, we shall be part of that great number who have been made perfect (Hebrews 12:23).

Today, as we live the life of faith, our Saviour, the Lord Jesus, sits at God's right hand upon his heavenly throne (Ephesians 1:20). We are all united to him through our faith, so we are able to say that even today we 'reign with Christ' (Ephesians 2:6; 2 Timothy 2:12).

However, the day is coming when we shall be glorified. This worn-out body of mine will be renewed and I shall have a glorious body like that of the Lord Jesus Christ after his resurrection. My heart and mind will have been cleansed of every last remnant of sin so that I shall at last be able to love and serve God perfectly in thought, word and deed.

When shall we be glorified? It will be completed when Christ returns and the souls of his people are reunited with their resurrected bodies. The judgement will take place and then Christ's people will be given their eternal home in the new heavens and new earth, where we shall see the face of God in Christ and there will be nothing to hurt us. There will be no more aches and pains, no more tears, no more unhappiness, no more death. There will be nothing there to cause distress of any kind. Why not? Because there will be no more sin. Sin is the cause of all our problems.

Are you looking forward to your glorification? If you belong to Christ then this will be the most wonderful day that is yet to be. And you will be glorified if you are one of those whom God 'foreknew'.

We have looked at the links in God's golden chain of salvation. Because God is all-powerful, his plan for us will surely come to pass. If you believe that you belong to Christ then check it out by examining your daily life. Is there evidence in your life and behaviour of a likeness to Christ? Are you obedient to the commands of God? Do you love God? Do you believe his promises? Here is the proof that you belong to the Saviour and will one day be glorified.

To think about

1. Do the Scriptures tell us when the Lord will return to earth? (Matthew 24:36).
2. How are we to prepare for his return? (2 Peter 3:10-14).
3. Make a list of the links in God's golden chain of salvation.

A Wonderful Future

They can't be found!

Read
• • • • • • • • • • • • • • • • • •
Amos 9:1-8

'"Can anyone hide himself in secret places, so I shall not see him?" says the LORD; "Do I not fill heaven and earth?" says the LORD' (Jeremiah 23:24).

We live in a world where there are many people who simply disappear without a trace. In some cases they can no longer cope with the life they are living, so they escape from it all and make a new start somewhere else. Others are criminals who do not want to be captured by the police, so move to a hiding-place. Then there are a few who have been murdered. There are just so many reasons why people disappear.

Australia is known worldwide for the Great Barrier Reef and recently this picturesque part of the world was the scene where two tourists disappeared. Most people who visit 'the Land Down Under' try to visit the area where the reef is found. The coral and the fish that live there produce a wonderful scene of colour and movement. Tourists are transported to the area where they are able to view the undersea world through glass-bottomed boats. Sometimes visitors put on scuba-diving gear and swim in the shallow water where there is an abundance of coral.

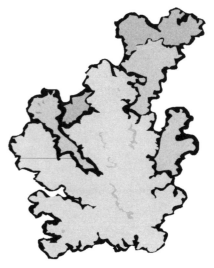

143

Some time ago a visiting couple went with many others on such a tour and when the boat returned home they were missing. At first it was assumed that the captain of the boat must somehow have over-looked the couple while they were swimming under water, leaving them behind accidentally. However, re-cently facts have been reported that raise the question: 'Did the young couple use the boat trip on purpose to stage their disappearance?' Maybe we shall never know the answer to this intriguing mystery.

As we read our Bibles we find that the word 'hide' occurs eighty times in the New King James Version. Adam and Eve fell into sin and when God came to speak to them they hid themselves. There is no doubt that sin cre-ates a barrier between God and the sinner. Moses' parents hid him from the Egyptians and later we read of David hiding from King Saul. Joseph and Mary hid Jesus in Egypt from King Herod's soldiers. And I feel sure that most people reading these words have been involved in hiding a couple of times — even if only while playing 'hide and seek'.

Our reading is about God's judgement upon the people of Israel who had turned their backs upon Jehovah, their covenant God. They were worship-ping false gods and living for pleasure. The Babylonians were to take the people into captivity for seventy years. This meant that they were to be forcibly removed from their homes and land and taken as captives to a strange

country. Try to imagine how you would have felt if you were there on the day the Assyrian armies appeared over the mountains. I am sure that you would have run as quickly as you could to a hiding-place. You would not have wanted to be taken captive!

However, God said that there would be no safe hiding-place. The Babylonians would search everywhere for the terrified people and take them captive. When I read those words I thought of the coming again of the Lord when everyone would be brought together before the judgement seat. Every person who ever walked the earth will be there.

In this passage we are taught that God is omnipresent. In other words, he is present in all parts of this universe and no one can escape his all-seeing eye: 'Behold, the eyes of the Lord GOD are on the sinful kingdom' (Amos 9:8). God could see all that was happening in sinful Israel, just as he sees the sins of all people everywhere.

When Christ returns, people who have not repented of their sins will try to hide from him in terror. John describes it like this in the book of Revelation: 'And the kings of the earth, the great men, the rich men, the commanders, the mighty men, every slave and free man, hid themselves in the caves and in the rocks of the mountains, and said to the mountains and rocks, "Fall on us and hide us from the face of him who sits on the throne and from the wrath of the Lamb! For the great day of his wrath has come, and who is able to stand?"' (Revelation 6:15-17).

All the powerful angels will gather everyone together to stand before Christ's judgement throne and there receive their just rewards — praise or condemnation.

In our Bible reading God ensured that some citizens of Israel were saved (Amos 9:8); there would be a remnant who would live to serve the Lord. Today too there are people in this world of sin who love God and live by faith in the Lord Jesus Christ. They are saved and will inherit the kingdom of heaven.

May none of us have reason to hide from the Lord on judgement day. We shall have no need, or wish, to do so if we know that our sins have been hidden from the eye of God by the sacrifice of the Lamb of God.

To think about

1. Why will sinners who have not repented fear meeting the Lamb of God?
2. Read Revelation 20:11-15. What is described in this passage of Scripture?
3. Why were the people of Judah *seventy* years in captivity? Read 2 Chronicles 36:21 and Leviticus 26:33-35.

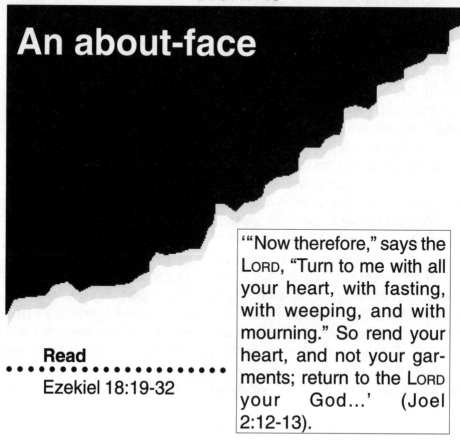

An about-face

Read
• • • • • • • • • • • • • • • • • • • •
Ezekiel 18:19-32

'"Now therefore," says the LORD, "Turn to me with all your heart, with fasting, with weeping, and with mourning." So rend your heart, and not your garments; return to the LORD your God...' (Joel 2:12-13).

The *Shorter Catechism* asks the question: 'What is repentance unto life?' (Question 87). The answer is given: 'Repentance unto life is a saving grace, whereby a sinner, out of a true sense of his sin, and apprehension of the mercy of God in Christ, does with grief and hatred of his sin, turn from it unto God, with full purpose of, and endeavour after, new obedience.' Today we will concentrate on the word 'turn'.

One day at school when I was a bit of a problem for my teacher, he said in a serious tone of voice, 'Cromarty, you'd better turn over a new leaf and in future do your homework. You've blotted your copybook.' I'm sure most people have tried at some time to 'turn over a new leaf' and start again. Our sins have created problems for us in our relationship with God. Many people have the idea that if they just forget the past and start again, all will be well.

A close friend of mine works among a very underprivileged group of people in Australia. He spends a lot of time travelling about the countryside, helping the pastors with their local congregations. He has a responsibility to care for the people spiritually as well as doing all he can to improve their living standards.

Many of the pastors with whom he works live in very harsh conditions in the Australian outback. He told me the story of one pastor who in his young days must have broken his parents' hearts with his sinful way of life. There were times when the police came knocking on their door demanding to know where their son could be found. One night the wayward son became involved in a fight and seriously injured the other person. He grabbed his bags and ran away.

Some years later, when he was down to his last cent, he made his way to a local church and there he listened to the good news of Christ, the Saviour of sinners. That night he called upon Jesus to forgive him his sins. He wept many tears over his sins, but he knew that they were forgiven. Sadly he couldn't go home to tell his godly parents the good news as they had died some years before. However, he cleaned himself up, dressed himself in decent clothes and found a job. Later he entered a theological college where he studied to become a pastor.

Years later he was back among the people he once knew, preaching Christ. They were amazed at the changes they saw in his life and asked him what had happened. He rejoiced at the opportunity to tell them that the Holy Spirit had given him a new heart that could love God. 'Now,' he said, 'I'm a new person. I don't just wear clean clothes, but I have the righteousness of Christ covering my sins.'

One day as he was driving along the road he was stopped by a policeman conducting a roadside check who asked him for his licence and breathalysed him. For some reason the policeman went to his car and checked the man's name with the head office. The result was that the pastor was arrested and charged with the assault that had taken place many years before. The police computer had not forgotten the warrant that still existed. After a time, however, when it was realized that a true change had taken place in the man, the warrant for his arrest was torn up.

Too often we read of people who continue to sin despite their confessions of sorrow. A thief was released from the court on condition that he would maintain good behaviour when he wept and told the magistrate that he was very sorry for his activities and had now changed his ways. Several weeks later he was back in court charged with theft and was sentenced to jail. He had shed tears, but his heart had not been changed. Only God can change the sinful heart!

God's people were facing an awful judgement because of their sins. They were wandering away from God and his righteousness. The prophet Joel, using the words of God, called them to repentance: 'Turn to me with all your heart … so rend your heart, and not your garments.' The people were called to 'turn' *from* their sins and return *to* God. It meant they were to turn around. But no one can turn from their sins unless God intervenes in that person's life. When the Holy Spirit takes up residence in the hearts of sinners they repent of their sins and turn around to face the God in whom they have saving faith. This action of turning around is called 'conversion'.

In our reading God calls his people to turn from their sins and obey his laws. Only this would save them from judgement. We read, '"For I have no pleasure in the death of one who dies," says the Lord GOD. "Therefore turn and live!"' (Ezekiel 18:32).

God says the same to all sinners: 'You will face condemnation unless you turn from your sins and live a life of faith in Christ.' Sinners love their sins and have no fear of God or judgement. Hatred of sin and obedience to God's law are marks of saving faith.

Have you been converted? Have you turned from your sins to Christ? If you are converted then thank God for changing your heart and making it possible for you to 'turn'.

May God bless you all with a love of the Lord Jesus Christ.

To think about

1. What is meant by the word 'conversion'?
2. What makes it possible for sinners to turn away from the sinful life they love?
3. What is meant by the words in today's text: 'So rend your heart, and not your garments'?

Things are not always what they seem

Read
• • • • • • • • • • • • • • • • • •
1 Peter 5:1-11

'Beware of false prophets, who come to you in sheep's clothing, but inwardly they are ravenous wolves' (Matthew 7:15).

There are many people and things that are not what they seem to be. I like chocolate and one day I bought some which I expected to be really delicious. The bar had a colourful wrapping, but when I opened it up I found some little creatures in the nuts. I returned the chocolate to the manufacturers who sent me a letter to say how sorry they were, as well as a small package of sweets.

One day at school a class was raising money to assist a sporting team who were to visit another school. The group of children decided to have a lamington sale. Now lamingtons are easy to make — they consist of small cubes (each side about 7.5 centimetres in length) of sponge cake, coated with chocolate icing and then sprinkled with white coconut. They look good and usually taste great. The children bought a couple of huge sponge cakes from the baker and cut them up at school, working in an

assembly line to make the lamingtons. Some children coated the blocks of cake with the soft chocolate icing while others splashed on the dry coconut. Another group packed them on plates ready for the sale.

However, there were a couple of humorists amongst the class and they had brought along several sponge rubber cubes. After carefully smothering them with chocolate coating and coconut they took them to the headmaster so he could taste the finished product.

I can still see the school principal graciously thanking the children for their kindness in giving him the first one to taste. Everyone who knew the joke was standing around watching. The headmaster sank his teeth into the 'lamington' and pulled his hand away from his mouth. The sponge rubber stretched as he tried to get it away from his lips. There was a very surprised look on his face when the 'lamington' slipped from his hand and sprung back into shape, hitting him on the mouth. A great cheer went up and the children began to laugh, with the principal joining in when he saw the joke.

It is so true that things are not always what they seem to be!

Through the ages God has placed people in positions of authority to care for his people. Spiritually, in the days of the Old Testament, God's people were ruled by men from the tribe of Levi. Today the church is governed by elders, or pastors (a name which comes from the Latin word for 'shepherds'). They have the responsibility of caring for the spiritual well-being of God's people — those who have been redeemed by the blood of the Lord Jesus. This means that Christians are very special people to God. Elders, then, must serve the Lord Jesus as 'under-shepherds' in charge of the flock (under the authority of the Lord Jesus, who is the 'Chief Shepherd' — see also John 10:1-30), not so that they will be praised or receive some special payment from the church, but simply because they love Christ and their brothers and sisters in the Lord.

In the various ages of the church there have been overseers of God's people who were hypocrites. God warned us of such people when he said these

men lead the covenant people astray: 'Woe to the shepherds of Israel who feed themselves! Should not the shepherds feed the flocks? ... My flock became food for every beast of the field, because there was no shepherd.' Then God's warning came loud and clear: 'I will require my flock at their hand' (Ezekiel 34:2,8,10).

Today we also hear of shepherds who do not care for the 'flock' of Christ. Some are more interested in making money and enjoying themselves than they are in caring for the people of God. Others deny the bodily resurrection of the Lord Jesus and treat Christ's miracles with scorn.

The apostle Peter wrote of the 'false prophets among the people'. They were the false teachers who taught false doctrine (2 Peter 2:1-3). Peter said that they were doomed. Today there are such people — men and women who teach lies. And what are we to do? First the apostle John said, 'Beloved, do not believe every spirit, but test the spirits, whether they are of God; because many false prophets have gone out into the world' (1 John 4:1). Then John went on to say that believers should examine closely the teachings of such people, comparing what they said with the Word of God. The apostle Paul and his companions praised the Bereans for judging his teachings by what the Scriptures said (Acts 17:11).

Many of these false prophets really believe that what they teach is truth. Unless God intervenes in their lives and opens their eyes to the truth, their end is hopeless, for Christ said of such people, 'For you travel land and sea to win one proselyte [i.e. follower], and when he is won, you make him twice as much a son of hell as yourselves' (Matthew 23:15).

Those 'lamingtons' were not what they seemed to be. Likewise there are some 'under-shepherds' who are wolves in sheep's clothing — they are not what they claim to be. Let us all make sure that we are not led astray by 'under-shepherds' who do not preach the true gospel, as it is found in the pages of Scripture. Let us thank God for those under-shepherds who genuinely care for the saints, faithfully serving the 'good Shepherd', the Lord Jesus Christ.

To think about

1. What is an 'under-shepherd'?
2. Why is Christ called 'the Good Shepherd'? (Read John 10:11).
3. What is the work of the church elders? (Read 1 Peter 5:1-4).
4. What is your responsibility to the elders, or leaders, of your congregation?

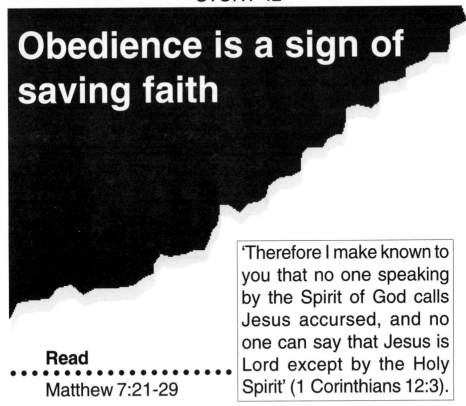

Obedience is a sign of saving faith

'Therefore I make known to you that no one speaking by the Spirit of God calls Jesus accursed, and no one can say that Jesus is Lord except by the Holy Spirit' (1 Corinthians 12:3).

Read

Matthew 7:21-29

Some people have the idea that they can accept Christ as Saviour without his also being their Lord. But this cannot be, because justification and sanctification go hand in hand. When the Holy Spirit calls a person to saving faith in Christ he or she shows that faith by true repentance of heart, calling upon the Lord Jesus for salvation. In the court of heaven the person is justified — forgiven and clothed in the righteousness of Christ. At the same time he or she is sanctified, which means set apart in Christ. The Christian is 'washed ... sanctified [and] ... justified in the name of the Lord Jesus and by the Spirit of our God' (1 Corinthians 6:11).

When we are 'sanctified', or set apart to serve God, the process begins by which the Holy Spirit undertakes the work of moulding the sinner into the likeness of the Saviour. In other words, just as Christ obeyed God, so also the justified sinner begins to obey God. True, there are disappointments and setbacks, but failures are followed by repentance and further struggles to live in a way which is pleasing to God. Obedience is hard work, but Christ must be both our Saviour and our Lord if our salvation is real. The two go together, as James wrote: 'Faith without works is dead' (James 2:20).

When Wags came to live at our home he had to be taught how to behave. We couldn't have put up with him if he didn't behave in an acceptable manner most of the time. So we taught him how to get up and down the steps.

'Sit!'

He was so small he could fit into my shoe and the steps were like a mountain to him. Then he had to be toilet-trained and taught how to 'shake hands' and 'sit'. He now knows what a lot of commands mean, plus the meaning of quite a few other words. If anyone mentions a 'ride in the car', he runs for his lead and jumps up on our bed so we can put his collar on his neck. He knows that he is not allowed in the car without his collar around his neck.

I have taught him to lie on his back when I say, 'Dead dog!' He must think this is stupid, but he does it to please his master. Sometimes he is disobedient and refuses to come when I call him, but he watches me and when I pick up a roll of paper or a stick he comes with his tail between his legs, watching out in case I am about to give him a slap.

When Val says, 'It's time for a bath' he sometimes hides under the settee and snarls at her as he doesn't like having a bath. He has been known to snarl at the grandchildren when, after a ride in the car, they try to lift him out. He loves to have a ride and likes to think that if he stays longer in the car he just might have another ride.

But, in general, Wags is obedient. I am the one who gives him his meals each day. I take him for a walk and play with him when I have the time and energy. Wags knows I am his master and he doesn't snarl at me when I tell him to get out of the car or that it's time for his bath.

To remain a member of the Cromarty family he has to be obedient and I'm sure he obeys because in his doggy way he loves us. I'm afraid that if he didn't obey (most of the time) life would become very trying for Wags.

When anyone is converted to Christ he or she becomes a new person. Once we were children of darkness, but following our new birth (the theological term is 'regeneration') we became children of light. Our heavenly

Father is light (1 John 1:5). When we are united to God's only begotten Son, who is 'the light of the world' (John 8:12), we are told to live 'as children of light' (Ephesians 5:8).

This means Christ is Lord of our lives and we obey him because we love him. Our text teaches us that it is only by the power of the indwelling Holy Spirit that we can call Jesus our Lord. This means that he is truly Lord of our lives and this is shown by our obedience to his commands, which we find in the Bible.

Our reading warns us that there are people who, when Christ returns, will claim to have called him 'Lord'. However, they did not mean what they said because they would not obey his commands. To call Christ 'Lord' and then to live a disobedient life is the work of a hypocrite or a very misguided person.

Christians should gladly and lovingly own Christ as their Lord and Saviour. The day is coming when all people will be brought to acknowledge that Christ is Lord. Paul wrote of that day, '... at the name of Jesus every knee [shall] bow, of those in heaven, and of those on earth, and of those under the earth, and ... every tongue ... confess that Jesus Christ is Lord, to the glory of God the Father' (Philippians 2:10-11).

May all who claim to be saved through faith in Christ, the Saviour, demonstrate that saving faith by their obedience to the commands of Jesus Christ, the Lord.

To think about

1. Why should God expect you to obey his commands?
2. We say that Christ is 'Lord'. What does this mean?
3. I have seen a talking bird. If it was taught to say, 'Christ is Lord', would it be saved? Explain the reasons for your answer.

The soap was cheap!

Read

••••••••••••••••••••

James 4:7-17

'He who has clean hands will be stronger and stronger' (Job 17:9).

I'm sure there are many of you who enjoy helping Mum and Dad, or someone you like, with the shopping. I have seen many mothers shopping with children in pushchairs and a couple more small children. In fact one day I told one mother who was struggling through a supermarket with a push-chair, two knee-high children and a shopping trolley partly filled with groceries, 'You deserve a medal!' She just said, 'Thanks! It's hard work.' While many children complain and make a noise there are many who are a real help to their mum or dad.

156

As I get older I find that when I go shopping with Val, I keep an eye out for bargains. 'Buy things you use when they are cheap,' is my motto. As a result my family tease me because one of the grandchildren discovered I had 152 rolls of toilet paper carefully packed away. Now when it's my birthday, I usually find a roll of toilet paper included with my gifts. Even Val has joined in the fun, giving me a roll of toilet paper covered with crossword puzzles.

A friend at church told me that his family were laughing at him for a similar reason. When he received $50 as his birthday gift his wife told him to buy something he liked. So down he went to the supermarket where he spied his favourite soap on a 'special'. He bought $50 worth of his soap. Now his wife and family joke about their 'soap-buying' husband and father.

Soap is important as we use it for cleaning. I guess most soaps would be used to keep our hands clean. The Scriptures have something to say about 'clean hands'. Job tells us that 'clean hands' will make us stronger and stronger. Now this does not mean that Job discovered a new method of exercise which would make his body stronger.

Washing hands has a spiritual significance. As we read the instructions given to the priests and people in the days of the Old Testament we find they were ordered to wash. Sometimes they had also to wash their clothes (Leviticus 15:8,10,11). The psalmist says that only those with 'clean hands and a pure heart' are fit to stand before God and worship him (Psalm 24:4).

We find in Exodus 40:30-32 the story of Moses and Aaron who were about to enter the tabernacle — the special tent where God met with his

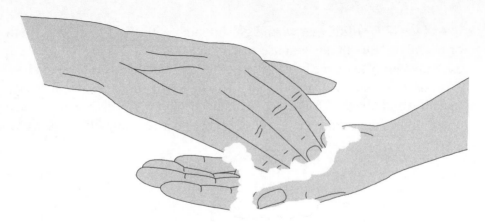

people and where sacrifices were offered in the days before the temple was built. We read, 'He ... put water there for washing; and Moses, Aaron, and his sons would wash their hands and their feet with water from it. Whenever they went into the tabernacle of meeting, and when they came near the altar, they washed, as the LORD had commanded Moses.' With all the washing carried out by the priests, their bodies, and especially their hands, must have been very clean when they carried out their duties.

Only those who are spiritually clean can worship God, and that work of cleansing comes from God alone. Following David's repentance he acknowledged that he needed to be made clean in his heart. He needed God to cleanse him, so he prayed, 'Purge me with hyssop, and I shall be clean; wash me, and I shall be whiter than snow' (Psalm 51:7).

The apostle John reminds us that this cleansing comes from the Holy Spirit's action in applying the benefits of Christ's redeeming work to the hearts of his people: '... and the blood of Jesus Christ his Son cleanses us from all sin... If we confess our sins, he is faithful and just to forgive us our sins and to cleanse us from all unrighteousness' (1 John 1:7,9).

Paul writes, 'Not by works of righteousness which we have done, but according to his mercy he saved us, through the washing of regeneration and renewing of the Holy Spirit' (Titus 3:5).

The offer of spiritual cleansing comes from God but so many reject it. They do not want to be spiritually clean. The writer to the Hebrews warned all professing Christians that they must remain faithful to the Lord and persevere to the end. Christ warned his disciples that they faced daily dangers when they preached the gospel: 'And you will be hated by all for my name's sake. But he who endures to the end will be saved' (Matthew 10:22).

To turn away and go back to the old, unclean, sinful ways is to invite God's anger: 'For if we sin wilfully after we have received the knowledge of the truth, there no longer remains a sacrifice for sins, but a certain fearful expectation of judgement, and fiery indignation, which will devour the adversaries... It is a fearful thing to fall into the hands of the living God' (Hebrews 10:26,27,31).

To think about

1. What is 'sanctification'? (The *Shorter Catechism* puts it like this: 'Sanctification is the work of God's free grace, whereby we are renewed in the whole man after the image of God, and are enabled more and more to die unto sin, and live unto righteousness' — Question 35).
2. In the Scriptures what does the command to 'cleanse your hands' (James 4:8) mean?
3. James tells his readers, 'Resist the devil and he will flee from you' (James 4:7). What does this mean?

My poor little cat

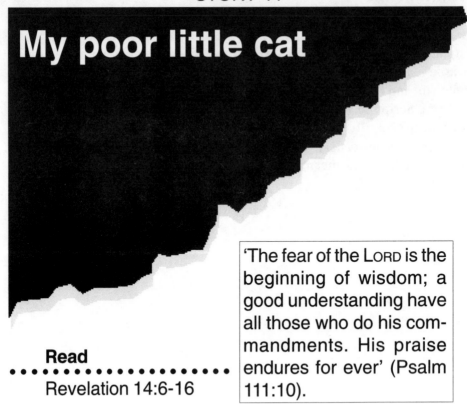

Read
● ● ● ● ● ● ● ● ● ● ● ● ● ● ● ● ● ● ● ●
Revelation 14:6-16

'The fear of the LORD is the beginning of wisdom; a good understanding have all those who do his commandments. His praise endures for ever' (Psalm 111:10).

There are so many people who have no fear of God. They go about their daily activities without a thought for God or his beloved Son. They receive wonderful blessings from the Lord yet never give thanks. We all experience difficult times but very few people stop to ask what lessons God has for them to learn in all this. There are some people who come along to worship on Sunday and the preaching of the Word has no effect upon them. Others, however, see their sins and turn to Christ for salvation.

I rejoice, even to this day, when I recall the Sunday night when a member of the congregation rang me to say that the Spirit of Christ had applied the sermon to his heart. He was weeping over his sins and rejoicing that now Christ was his Saviour. I'm sure that everyone who witnesses to someone else about the saving work of Christ would be overjoyed to hear of the salvation of that person.

One day a very close friend, who is the pastor of a congregation, told me of a man who came to him after the service with tears running down his cheeks. The sermon had warned unconverted people to repent of their sins and turn to Christ for forgiveness. Death had been mentioned, both physical death and spiritual death. It was a hard-hitting sermon and many people took the message to heart, examining themselves to be sure that they had true saving faith in Christ.

However, this man was so sad and there was no doubt that he was greatly distressed. The minister was rejoicing in his heart as the man seemed to be deeply concerned about his sins and his standing with God. He was repeating the words: 'Death is so awful, so terrible!'

Accompanying him into a small room, the pastor agreed with him that death was frightening because it ushered the sinner into judgement. He reminded the man that everyone would one day die, but as today was still the day of salvation he encouraged the man to put his trust in the Lord Jesus.

To those words the man replied in a surly tone of voice, 'Oh, I wasn't thinking about my death, but my poor little pet cat. He is getting old and has been so ill that I've made arrangements for the vet to put him down. Tomorrow I have to take him to the surgery. I don't know how I will cope. Death is so awful, so dreadful!'

The man was totally unconcerned about the standing of his own never-dying soul before God. His were not tears of repentance, but human sorrow for his pet cat which, like all animals, had no immortal soul. Now I can understand people feeling sorrow when a special pet dies, but it is so sad when people have no fear of death and the judgement which they must face.

They have no fear of God — in fact their motto is usually: 'Let us eat and drink, for tomorrow we die!' (1 Corinthians 15:32). This was the attitude of the rich man in the parable spoken by Christ (Luke 12:16-21). He was unconcerned about his standing before God. All he wanted was to enjoy his retirement. Maybe he too was concerned about the well-being of one of his pet animals. Suddenly God called him to judgement. The truth then burst upon his heart and he found it was then too late for repentance.

What is your standing before God? Are you ready for the Day of Judgement? It is a meeting you cannot escape. I pray that there will be tears of repentance in your eyes, and tears of sorrow because men and women do not keep God's law. Remember, there is a day coming for all who have repented of their sins and trusted in Christ when all tears will be wiped away by God. Pay attention to the words of Scripture, and to the teaching you hear from the Bible in church or Sunday School, and make sure you have made preparations for the day of your death. Faith in the Lord Jesus Christ is the only way by which you may avoid what is described in today's reading.

To think about

1. Read Revelation 14:13 and discuss what it is teaching.
2. Why is death called an 'enemy'?
3. Why do people die?
4. Why did Christ say that the rich man was a 'fool'? (Read Luke 12:16-21).

Thanks! You may come again

Read
••••••••••••••••••
Psalm 107:1-9

'It is good to give thanks to the LORD, and to sing praises to your name, O Most High...' (Psalm 92:1).

All people, even unbelievers, owe thanks to the Lord for his goodness to them. As we look around each day we see much happiness in the world. The Scriptures remind us that 'He makes his sun rise on the evil and on the good, and sends rain on the just and on the unjust' (Matthew 5:45). Yet so many never think to give thanks to God for his great goodness.

There are many incidents in the Bible where people gave thanks to the Lord for his loving-kindness to them. In 1 Chronicles 16 we read a psalm of David in which he gave thanks to God for his goodness in having the ark of the covenant returned to the tabernacle in Jerusalem. The psalm opens with the words: 'Oh, give thanks to the LORD!' Then, after recalling many instances of the Lord's goodness to them, David exclaims once again, 'Oh, give thanks to the LORD, for he is good! For his mercy endures for ever' (1 Chronicles 16:8,34).

I wonder just how many times you have thanked your parents and other people for their kindness and help to you. Maybe you should take more notice of the good things they do for you and make the effort to say, 'Thank you!' more often.

Some time ago my brother saw a large field of almost 100 acres that looked as if it might be a place where gold could be found. It was well-fenced, and on a hill overlooking the land there was a house. John knew he couldn't just crawl through the fence and start searching for gold — he had to ask permission to enter the property. So he made his way to the house and knocked on the door. The lady owner opened the door and asked, 'Well, how can I help you?'

John explained that he was a Presbyterian minister who on his day off searched for gold. Then he asked the lady if he could use his metal detector to search parts of the field for those elusive gold nuggets. She was very happy to give John permission to spend the day wandering about, looking for gold.

At the end of the day when John had ten or twelve rather small golden nuggets in his pouch he decided to return to the lady and thank her for her kindness in allowing him to spend the day exploring her field. When she came to the door John handed her a small piece of gold and said, 'Thanks! I had an enjoyable day. Here's a sample of the gold I found.'

The lady was clearly surprised 'You're the first person to come back and say, "Thanks,"' she told John. 'And this is the first piece of gold from my land that I've ever seen. Thank you very much. Come back any time you like.'

Kindness deserves thanks.

The Lord Jesus met ten men whom he healed from the terrible disease of leprosy. These men, because of their illness, were not allowed to attend worship or mix with other citizens in case they passed the disease on to them. Everywhere they went they had to say, 'Unclean,' as a warning to people who came near. Life was very miserable for them.

Of the ten lepers healed by the Lord only one bothered to return to say, 'Thank you!' He bowed down before Christ because he was so thankful when he found his flesh was once again perfectly free from sores. Nine of the lepers were Jews and one was a Samaritan. It was this Samaritan who returned to say, 'Thank you' to Christ. What made this most unusual was that the Samaritans and the Jews had nothing to do with each other.

Christians have been cleansed of that awful disease, sin. If you have repented of your sins and confessed them to God, seeking his forgiveness, you have something for which to praise God. Thank God for his goodness to you — for the great blessings that are yours today and those that you will enjoy in the world to come.

We should also thank God for other people. Paul reminded the Ephesian Christians: 'I ... do not cease to give thanks for you, making mention of you in my prayers' (Ephesians 1:16).

In Psalm 107, from which today's reading was taken, we find the words, 'Oh, give thanks to the LORD for he is good!' repeated many times throughout the psalm. The psalmist was praising God and giving thanks for his protective care of Israel over many, many years and his goodness to them in many different situations.

I'm sure we all have a lot for which to thank God — as well as the people who love us and care for us. Don't forget to show your appreciation for everything they have done by saying, 'Thank you'.

To think about

1. When was the last time you said, 'Thank you' to someone for a kind act?
2. What has your mum or dad done for you lately for which you should give thanks?
3. Who were the Samaritans?
4. What has God done for you? Have you ever thanked him for his goodness?

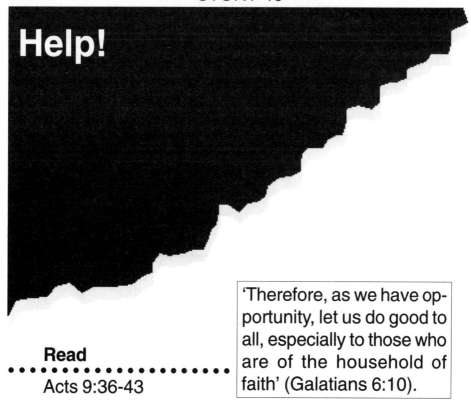

Help!

Read
• • • • • • • • • • • • • • • • • •
Acts 9:36-43

'Therefore, as we have opportunity, let us do good to all, especially to those who are of the household of faith' (Galatians 6:10).

There are many Bible stories about people who helped others. The command of God is that we are to help other people, and this means all people, not just our fellow Christians. Christ told the parable of the Good Samaritan in which he commanded everyone to care for people who need help.

The Lord Jesus set the example to his disciples, showing them how they were to act, when he knelt down and washed their dirty, smelly feet (John 13:1-5). He did not 'come to be served, but to serve' (Mark 10:45). Then he told them to do the same for others who were in need of help: 'For I have given you an example, that you should do as I have done to you' (John 13:15). Sometimes assisting other people is difficult and unpleasant, but Christ has commanded every one of his people to be a servant.

Some time ago a lady I know took her two children to the local supermarket to buy the week's groceries. With two little children at her feet what should have been a pleasant activity was hard work. She was always very pleased to get home. When her husband returned home after work he found her tired and worn out from the day's activities.

One evening he was met by his wife and children, all of whom were very excited. Shopping had been very exciting! They had been able to help someone who was really in need. An old lady who was doing her weekly shopping decided that she would tidy up her shopping trolley. As she was leaning

over she toppled forward and ended up head down in the trolley, unable to pull herself out.

The children were very excited as they told the story: 'Dad, she was upside down and couldn't get out! We had to pull her legs to get her out!'

Dad said he thought the family was pulling his leg!

The lady was not injured in her fall, but felt very embarrassed by what had happened.

Helping is the way we show our love to others. In the same way we show that we love the Lord Jesus.

Our reading was about a woman named Dorcas of whom the Scriptures record: 'This woman was full of good works and charitable deeds which she did.' Her death came as a sad blow to those who knew her because she was greatly loved, especially by those she had helped. When Peter arrived on the scene the weeping people showed him the clothing that Dorcas had made for them. God performed a great miracle through Peter when she was raised from the dead.

There are many people who need our help and encouragement. Think for a moment of all those senior citizens who lead a lonely life in their homes. Their children have grown up and moved away. Maybe they don't have many friends who are still alive. You have a wonderful opportunity to be a friend to some of those people. Visiting the sick in hospital is another good work. There are just so many ways we can help needy people.

Then there are the men and women who have been workers for the Lord in a special way and now are old and retired. We must never forget these people. Maybe you have retired missionaries living close to you. Having lived overseas for most of their lives they may not have many close friends. Visit them and let them know that you care for them. When the apostle Paul wrote to the Philippians he mentioned some who had laboured in gospel work: 'Help these women who laboured with me in the gospel, with Clement also, and the rest of my fellow workers, whose names are in the Book of Life' (Philippians 4:3).

We should also remember that when the difficult days come we have one who is ready and willing to help us — the Lord Jesus Christ. The writer to the Hebrews said, 'Let us therefore come boldly to the throne of grace, that we may obtain mercy and find grace to help in time of need' (Hebrews 4:16).

The Lord Jesus helps his people defeat the power of sin in their lives. He helped them spiritually in that he won salvation for them. Today from heaven he pours blessings upon all whose names have been written in the Book of Life. Let us all follow in his footsteps and do good to all.

To think about

1. In what way had Dorcas been a help to those in need?
2. What is a miracle?
3. Take out your atlas and find the towns mentioned by Luke in this story.
4. In what way does your church help needy people?

I felt terrible!

Read
• • • • • • • • • • • • • • • • • • • •
Ruth 2:14-23

'If any of you lacks wisdom, let him ask of God, who gives to all liberally and without reproach, and it will be given to him' (James 1:5).

There are times when something embarrasses us. There are also occasions when we do or say something that embarrasses other people. Often we just speak without thinking, which shows a great lack of wisdom. In his epistle James advises his Christian readers that they must pray to God asking for a wise nature. Then they will do and say things that glorify God and are not hurtful to others.

Our reading is about a woman named Ruth who came from Moab. She had married Mahlon, the son of Naomi, who with her husband Elimelech had migrated to that land in a time of severe famine. Naomi had been a widow for a long time and when Mahlon died — as well as her other son who had married another local girl, Orpah — she decided to return to Israel. After saying 'Goodbye' to all her friends, she prepared to part from her two daughters-in-law, but Ruth insisted that she would accompany Naomi on her return to Israel.

Ruth was determined to go with Naomi for one very important reason which we can see in her words:

Entreat me not to leave you,
Or to turn back from following after you;
For wherever you go, I will go;

And wherever you lodge, I will lodge;
Your people shall be my people,
And your God, my God.
Where you die, I will die,
And there will I be buried.
The LORD do so to me, and more also,
If anything but death parts you and me

(Ruth 1:16-17).

The key words are: 'Your God [shall be] my God.' Ruth had come to realize that the God whom Naomi worshipped, the God of Israel, was the true God and she turned her back on the pagan gods of her native Moab.

So Ruth left her homeland to return to Israel with Naomi. There she met Boaz who later became her husband. It was part of God's plan that Ruth and Boaz would become ancestors of the Lord Jesus.

Ruth went to the fields owned by Boaz to glean some of the grain that fell to the ground when the harvesting was being carried out. The poor citizens were entitled to gather ('glean') the grains of wheat, barley or other crops that the men working in the field had missed.

It was Boaz who told his workers to allow Ruth to glean among the sheaves of grain. In addition he told them not to embarrass her. The word used in the Scriptures here means just that — embarrass, or shame or humiliate. The young men would probably have made fun of Ruth as she gathered the grain. Boaz was not going to allow that to happen, so he warned the men to treat her with respect.

Read the book of Ruth. It is a lovely story of God's dealings with Naomi and Ruth. It is a love story which tells how Boaz fell in love with Ruth and married her.

We shouldn't embarrass anyone. I can still remember one night causing one of my daughters to be very embarrassed.

It was the time of the evening worship service and the members of the congregation were paying careful attention as I read the Scriptures. Then through the open church door I noticed our Cathie's pet cat. Continuing to read the words in the Bible with one eye, I kept the other on the cat. Sox saw a lot of legs and began to stroll through the seated congregation. Now and again he stopped to look up at me. He knew my voice well, of course. Then he made his way down the aisle and walked up into the pulpit, where he sat and gazed up into my face. I could see smiles on the faces of some of the people in the congregation.

When the cat jumped up on the chair beside me I knew something had to be done. I stopped reading and turned to grab Sox, who then decided he was not going to be caught. He jumped down from the chair to the pulpit floor. By now a lot more people were smiling as they sat watching to see what I was going to do next. As I tried to catch the cat he jumped from the pulpit to the table below and there he sat. Some of the congregation were no longer smiling — they were laughing out loud.

At that point I just gave up, and asked Cathie to come out and collect her pet. Poor Cathie felt so embarrassed as she came to the front of the building and called, 'Puss, puss! Come here, Sox.'

Fortunately Sox went to Cathie and she removed the uninvited visitor from the building. Then we were able to continue with our service of worship, but even to this day Cathie reminds me of the night Sox caused her such embarrassment. In future, he was locked in the garage during the time of the evening service.

We should be careful to avoid embarrassing people, but instead should show kindness and consideration to them in the words we speak and the things we do. The writer of the Proverbs said, 'Get wisdom! Get understanding!' (Proverbs 4:5).

May God be pleased to bless us in our dealings with people so that we cause them no hurt. Let the world see true Christian love in all we do and say.

To think about

1. What was 'gleaning'?
2. What was God's purpose in the gleaning laws?
3. Who were the descendants of Boaz and Ruth? (See Ruth 4:13-22; Matthew 1:5).
4. Ruth came from the land of Moab. From whom were these people descended? (Read Deut. 2:9; Gen. 11:27).

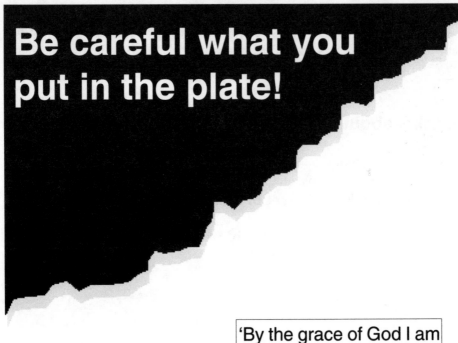

Be careful what you put in the plate!

Read
• •
Daniel 4:28-37

'By the grace of God I am what I am...' (1 Corinthians 15:10).

There are many proud people in the world. These people enjoy boasting about their possessions and what they have accomplished. They think they are better than other people and have the habit of 'looking down' on others. They like to boast that they have gained their wealth by their own efforts. The Lord has a warning for all these people. To the Israelites he said, '[Beware lest] you say in your heart, "My power and the might of my hand have gained me this wealth." And you shall remember the LORD your God, for it is he who gives you power to get wealth...' (Deuteronomy 8:17-18).

There are some people who don't want others to think they are just ordinary people and do all they can to give everyone the impression that they are important or wealthy. The writer of the Proverbs says, 'There is one who makes himself rich, yet has nothing; and one who makes himself poor, yet has great riches' (Proverbs 13:7).

The apostle Paul knew that all his abilities came from the God of grace. He wrote, 'Who makes you differ from another? And what do you have that you did not receive? Now if you did indeed receive it, why do you boast as if you had not received it?' (1 Corinthians 4:7). This is why he wrote those humbling words: 'But by the grace of God I am what I am...' (1 Corinthians 15:10). Each one of us should remember these words because they apply to us as well.

174

Some people have the idea that it is by doing good deeds that they will earn their salvation. They reason like this: 'If I obey God's law to the best of my ability and always do good to other people, God will have to save me. I will have earned God's love and he will have to reward me.' Because Paul knew that there would be people who thought this way he wrote, 'For by grace you have been saved through faith, and that not of yourselves; it is the gift of God, not of works, lest anyone should boast' (Ephesians 2:8-9).

I once knew an old lady — in fact I lived in her home for two years while I attended teachers' training college. She was a great cook and always made sure I was very well fed. She kept the home spotless, but she was a very proud lady.

She was a widow who owned her own home, but didn't want anyone to know she was receiving the old age pension. She wanted people to think she had plenty of money and didn't depend upon the government for support. I feel sure that everyone knew she was getting the old age pension, but she just wouldn't admit it to her friends. No, she was proud and wanted to have people believe she was well-to-do.

The church she attended asked all the members of the congregation to promise to give regularly to the collection. In that way the deacons could plan for the future as they would know what money could be expected each week. They gave all the members a packet of small envelopes in which they could place their promised collection. Each week the lady faithfully put her money in the envelope and when the deacons came around during the service she placed her envelope carefully on the plate.

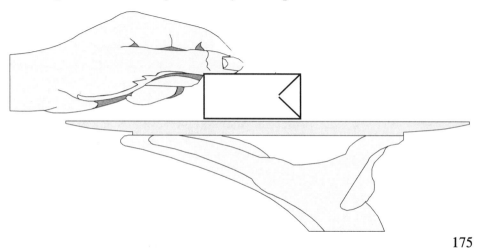

Her eyesight was failing and one Sunday morning as the plate came round she fumbled in her handbag, looking for the envelope. Taking from her bag what she thought was the envelope containing her money, she carefully placed it on the collection plate. But try to imagine her shock, horror and surprise when one of the deacons approached her after the service and handed her back her pension card. The poor lady had mistakenly placed the pension card on the plate, revealing to everyone her true situation. The dear lady felt so embarrassed and shamed by the incident that she said she could never again hold up her head.

Now there is no shame in receiving a pension from the government. Governments should care for the elderly as well as people who can't look after themselves. The Bible warns us all: 'Pride goes before destruction, and a haughty spirit before a fall,' and 'A man's pride will bring him low' (Proverbs 16:18; 29:23).

Think for a moment of that proud Babylonian king, Nebuchadnezzar. He boasted to everyone that he had made the city of Babylon by his own might and power: 'Is not this great Babylon, that I have built for my royal dwelling by my mighty power and for the honour of my majesty' (Daniel 4:30). Then in a moment of time God made him insane and for seven years Nebuchadnezzar wandered about in the fields eating grass with the cattle. He was a pitiful sight.

Today's reading tells the story of Nebuchadnezzar's restoration to good health. He acknowledged that God was the ruler of the universe and all the glory of Babylon came from God alone. I often wonder about that proud king who was humbled by God. Maybe one day we shall meet him in heaven because he acknowledged Jehovah to be God. He said, 'Now I, Nebuchadnezzar, praise and extol and honour the King of heaven, all of whose works are truth, and his ways justice. And those who walk in pride he is able to put down' (Daniel 4:37).

Satan's sin was pride. He wanted to occupy the throne of God (Isaiah 14:13-14). Eve's sin was pride. She also believed Satan's lies that if she ate from the tree of the knowledge of good and evil she would be 'like God, knowing good and evil' (Genesis 3:5).

We are warned in Scripture to control our tongues, because it is with our words that we boast. We read that 'The tongue is a little member [of the body] and boasts great things' (James 3:5).

If you want to boast then do what the psalmist recommended: 'In God we boast all day long, and praise your name for ever' (Psalm 44:8). If we want to praise anyone then let us glorify the Lord (2 Corinthians 10:17).

Pride is a horrible sin and the truth is that no one has anything of which he or she can boast. Everything we have comes from our God of grace. Thank him for all he has done for you and work hard, making good use of his gracious gifts.

To think about

1. What special talents do you have?
2. How do you use these gifts to the glory of God?
3. Proud, boastful people are not very likeable. How do you cope with such people?
4. List some things the Lord hates (Read Proverbs 6:16-19).

Better late than never

Read
• • • • • • • • • • • • • • • • • • •
Luke 23:39-43

'Behold, now is the ac-
cepted time; behold, now
is the day of salvation'
(2 Corinthians 6:2).

It is so easy to forget an important date.
I'm sure there are many of my readers
who have been embarrassed because
of their bad memories.

One Sunday as I was preaching a
thought flashed into my mind. It is
strange how our brains work. I was
concentrating on presenting the gospel when, as I looked around the congregation, I saw Val and the thought
came to my mind: 'Today is our wedding anniversary and I forgot.' I
couldn't stop preaching, but as soon
as I had a moment to think I began to
wonder what excuse I could make. I
thought, 'She is just so kind. She has
let the day pass without reminding me
how forgetful I am.'

As soon as I had the opportunity I
stammered out, 'Val, I'm so sorry, but

178

I forgot…' However, it was wonderful to hear her reply, 'You forgot what?' It was then I realized she too had forgotten our wedding anniversary. We both had a laugh and the next day had a special meal out. Yes, it is better to do the right thing late than never.

Some people rarely forget anything, but they have the bad habit of putting things off till another day. There are too many people who, when they hear the good news of peace between God and man, say they will think about it later. The Lord has something to say to those people: 'Behold, now is the accepted time; behold, now is the day of salvation' (2 Corinthians 6:2).

Once I was asked by a friend to visit a seriously ill lady who was in hospital. My friend was concerned about the state of her friend's relationship with Christ. She knew the seriousness of sin and that there was a Saviour who welcomed sinners who repented. When I reached the lady's bedside she was connected to many tubes, had an oxygen mask over her face and was heavily drugged. I tried to speak to her, but it was too late. She couldn't hear what I was saying and spent most of the time just moaning in distress. When I walked out of the hospital I was so upset I drove home and sat down and prayed. The lady

died several days later and for her I don't think there was any 'Better late than never'.

The writer to the Hebrews had a serious warning to those who put off their salvation: 'How shall we escape if we neglect so great a salvation...?' (Hebrews 2:3). No one should put off going to Christ and seeking salvation. Tomorrow may well be too late.

Nevertheless, there is a story in the Bible which should give everyone hope that salvation is freely available to those who repent, right up to the point of death.

Christ had been nailed to a cross and there he hung between two other condemned men. They were both suffering punishment for their crimes. Christ, the innocent Son of God, was hanging there on the cross bearing the sins of his people — suffering in their place the punishment of a God whose holy nature is offended by sin. All three were facing the reality of a very painful death.

Think of it — there was Jesus Christ, nailed to a cross, naked, bleeding, with perspiration on his face and covered with dirt and dust. I don't think he looked like a king of any kind. Kings don't usually hang on crosses but rather sit on thrones in palaces. However, that thief looked at Jesus and made a request: 'Lord, remember me when you come into your kingdom' (Luke 23:42).

The Holy Spirit had touched the man's heart just a short time before he died. He simply looked to Jesus, hanging on the cross, and there found salvation. He had probably been one of those people who had the attitude that says, 'Eat, drink and be merry, for tomorrow we die.' No doubt he had heard of Christ. Maybe he had seen his miracles and heard him speak, but he didn't believe — not until the last hours of his life. For that thief on the cross it certainly was 'Better late than never'.

Another man who neglected his salvation was King Agrippa. Paul, who was on trial because of his Christian testimony, had spoken publicly of the saving work of Christ and the need of repentance. Then he issued a personal challenge to the king. But Agrippa replied, as he turned his back on the gospel preached by Paul, 'You almost persuade me to become a Christian' (Acts 26:28).

I remind you all that today is the day of salvation. For many there may be no tomorrow.

To think about

1. 'Today you will be with me in Paradise' (Luke 23:43). Where and what is Paradise?
2. There are some people who teach that when we die our souls go to sleep until Christ returns and wakes us up. Prove this belief to be wrong from today's passage.
3. Find other passages of Scripture which teach that when Christians die they immediately pass into the presence of the Lord Jesus (see Acts 7:59; Philippians 1:21,23).

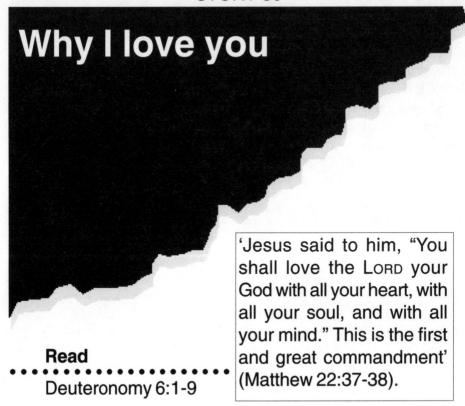

Why I love you

Read
• •
Deuteronomy 6:1-9

'Jesus said to him, "You shall love the LORD your God with all your heart, with all your soul, and with all your mind." This is the first and great commandment' (Matthew 22:37-38).

The covenant people of Israel sang with joy the wonderful words of the psalmist: 'I love the LORD, because he has heard my voice …' (Psalm 116:1). Here was a man who had a reason for loving God.

I would like to ask you two questions. First, do you love God? Secondly, if your answer to the first question is, 'Yes', why do you love God?

One day a proud Pharisee, a lawyer by profession, who had seen Christ silence the Sadducees, believed he could call the Lord's wisdom into question. He asked, 'Teacher, which is the great commandment in the law?' To this question the Lord replied, '"You shall love the LORD your God with all your heart, with all your soul, and with all your mind." This is the first and great commandment. And the second is like it: "You shall love your neighbour as yourself." On these two commandments hang all the Law and the Prophets' (Matthew 22:36-40).

I believe there are two great reasons why Christians love God. The first is because of all he has done for them in the Lord Jesus Christ. The second is because of his character — the qualities which are often referred to as his 'attributes' (e.g. goodness, holiness etc.)

In our human relationships some people become our very close friends. Maybe some of the parents who are reading these words can say that they married one of those people who became a very good friend.

When I first met my wife, Val, I saw someone who just looked attractive. I was soon to find out, however, that she was also a very kind person who was always ready to give me help. If I needed a book for my studies she seemed to know where I could find it. When she found out that I enjoyed chocolate-malted milk-shakes, she occasionally bought me one. Before we were married, when I had to teach at a school far away it was Val who wrote to me each week and looked forward to seeing me three times a

year during the school holidays. We didn't own a car and the distance between us was too great to meet at weekends. We just saw one another every three months. But Val was always there to encourage me. I loved her because of what she did for me.

There was a second reason why I loved her, and that was because of her nature. She was quiet and had a very kind nature, always ready to help anyone she could. I found out that she was dependable and very patient. There were many other aspects of her character that made me love her more and more.

Christians love God, first of all, because of all that he has done for them in Christ. God, in his great love and mercy, showed us our sins and the spiritual danger we were in. The Holy Spirit changed the hearts of all those whom God 'foreknew' (or 'foreloved'). We saw that we were at risk of spending eternity banished from God's presence. John Bunyan described the world in which sinners lived as the 'City of Destruction'. However, God

intervened. We read, 'And the LORD your God will circumcise your heart … to love the LORD your God with all your heart and with all your soul, that you may live' (Deuteronomy 30:6). We became new creatures in the Lord Jesus. The Spirit of Christ indwelt our hearts and gave us a saving faith in Christ through which all the divine blessings could flow to us.

We saw the love of God in the Lord Jesus, the sinless sin-bearer, suspended between heaven and earth upon a Roman cross with his life saving-blood pouring from his broken body. Tears of love and gratitude flowed from our eyes as the understanding burst upon our hearts and minds: 'My sins did that to the Son of God!' And when we heard that awful cry from the cross, 'My God, my God, why have you forsaken me?' (Matthew 27:46) love blossomed in our hearts. Our Lord was forsaken, tasting the pains of hell for his people, that they might never be forsaken. We rejoice, knowing that Christ won for us the righteousness we need to enter heaven and stand in the presence of the eternal God.

There is a second reason why we love God. Our love grows stronger each day as we discover more about his character, or attributes. His holiness fills us with awe and wonder, while his plan of salvation is a magnificent display of his mercy. Our hearts are filled with love as we meditate upon his abounding grace, love and mercy. The words of David are a cause for rejoicing:

> The LORD is merciful and gracious,
> Slow to anger, and abounding in mercy…
> He has not dealt with us according to our sins,
> Nor punished us according to our iniquities.
> For as the heavens are high above the earth,
> So great is his mercy toward those who fear him
>
> (Psalm 103:8-11).

We discovered that our God is immutable — he cannot change. This means we can trust all his promises. He has promised that he will never leave us and that all who place their faith in his Son will be saved; that no one can snatch us from the hands of the Saviour — we are eternally secure.

Our salvation is all of God. His gracious love has delivered us from everlasting punishment and opened wide the doors of heaven to his people. The Lord bids us welcome. Our hearts are overflowing with love for Christ and the desire to be with Christ. There is a longing to walk the golden streets of heaven and gaze upon the face of 'the Son of God, who loved [us] and gave himself for [us]' (Galatians 2:20). We are humbled greatly in the knowledge that everything we have and will ever have comes from God — we are what we are by the grace of the God of grace.

If you are a Christian, then, by your life and words, show this sin-sick world that you love God. Only Christians can rejoice because they are members of the kingdom of heaven, whose Lord is 'King of kings and Lord of lords' (Revelation 19:16).

To think about

1. Why should Christians love God?
2. Who is God?
3. Name someone you love and explain why it is you love that person.

You shouldn't be up there! Get down!

Read
• • • • • • • • • • • • • • • • • •
1 Kings 11:1-10

'Do not enter the path of the wicked, and do not walk in the way of evil. Avoid it, do not travel on it; turn away from it and pass on' (Proverbs 4:14-15).

All who belong to Christ have the desire to live a holy life because they want to be like their Saviour. The Holy Spirit is working to make us more like Christ because this is one of the great purposes of salvation: we are 'predestined to be conformed to the image of his [God's] Son' (Romans 8:29). This means that we ourselves must also make the effort to avoid sin.

Our text and reading give us very good advice — do not follow the way of life of worldly people; avoid as much as possible close involvement and companionship with people who do not

fear God or live in a way that pleases him. We should not be found in those places where God has forbidden us to be. As Christians we must exert an influence for good in the world. We are to be salt and light, witnessing to Christ's salvation. We are not therefore meant to shut ourselves away completely from all contact with people who are not Christians. However, great care must be taken to avoid being contaminated by the outlook and behaviour of the unbelieving world around us.

In my younger days I had surgery and was forced to spend three weeks in hospital. For two of those weeks I was confined to my bed. I was not even permitted to put my feet to the floor. As the surgery was extensive I didn't feel like moving. I was happy to obey the doctor's instructions. Then there was the hospital matron, who had a loud voice! All the nurses obeyed her and the patients were very careful not to annoy her. She was a tyrant!

Eventually I was allowed to get out of bed and sit in a chair, and I found this the opportunity to play a joke or two on some of the other patients. I wanted to cheer them up. When they went to the bathroom I would put something under their sheets to make it uncomfortable for them when they went back to bed.

When I saw a man I knew well going to the bathroom, I went into the matron's small office, climbed up on her table and looked over the wall, which did not reach the ceiling. I had a glass partly filled with cold water and was just about to toss the water over the man, when in walked the matron and found me where I should not have been. She didn't say very much, but what she did say made me get down from her table and go back to bed. I certainly behaved myself after that, and when my doctor called in to see me he told me that if I didn't take care I would be confined to bed for the remainder of my hospital stay.

There are many times when we find ourselves in places where we should not be, and this causes great distress to our parents, teachers and others.

This is what our text teaches us. If we belong to Christ then we should not make close friends with the ungodly. Just spending time in the company of ungodly people means they might influence us to sin. Walking with people who do not fear God — that is, going about with them as one of the group — may well lead to our becoming involved in their sinful activities. We could become interested in their worldly ways and begin to show an interest in their lifestyle. The final step is to sit with such people, which means we now delight in their sinful ways and become involved in activities that bring shame upon our profession of faith in Christ (read Psalm 1:1).

All who love God should seek companionship among and fellowship with his people, who help us to live the life of holiness.

King Solomon started so well. He expressed his love for God, built the temple and encouraged the people to serve the Lord. But he became involved with ungodly women who turned his heart away from God. He disobeyed the command of God and put himself in a situation where he should not have been. We read, 'When Solomon was old ... his wives turned his heart after other gods; and his heart was not loyal to the Lord his God, as was the heart of his father David' (1 Kings 11:4).

Lot chose to settle in the area near the city of Sodom. He placed himself in a situation where he should not have been and it wasn't long before he was living in Sodom itself. We read of Sodom, 'But the men of Sodom were exceedingly wicked and sinful against the Lord' (Genesis 13:13). The life of Lot and his family turned out to be a tragedy and there can be no doubt that this was due to the fact that he chose to live among the ungodly — he sat down with them.

How often it is that we pray that we should not be led into temptation, and then put ourselves in places and with people where we are surrounded with temptations. By our actions we mock what we say in our prayers.

The apostle Paul wrote, 'For what fellowship has righteousness with lawlessness? And what communion has light with darkness? ... Therefore "Come out from among them and be separate," says the Lord. "Do not touch what is unclean, and I will receive you"' (2 Corinthians 6:14,17).

We must always be careful to avoid people and situations that are likely to cause us to fall into sin. Make sure that you are not be found in any place where you could not take the Lord, or where he would not be found.

To think about

1. List some places where it is good to be.
2. Make a list of places which it is best to avoid.
3. Read Psalm 1:1 and discuss what it is teaching.
4. Who are your best friends and why is that so?

It's now a lovely tree

Read

•••••••••••••••••••••

Isaiah 11:1-10

'There shall come forth a Rod from the stem of Jesse, and a Branch shall grow out of his roots' (Isaiah 11:1).

I have seen forests that have been cut down and left for years. Many of the tree-stumps are dead and the wood has rotted away. However, every now and again I saw a green shoot appear from the base of one of these trees and before too long a small tree was growing out of what appeared to be a dead tree-stump. The truth is that the stump still had a little bit of life in it.

One winter Val planted two new trees in our garden. Occasionally we have a frost and to protect one tree she decided to put a black plastic bag over it each night. In this way she expected to prevent any damage caused by a frost. On the night following the planting we had a very severe frost which I thought would have killed both trees. When we opened the back door to look at our trees we

189

were sure one had been badly damaged. However, we felt hopeful that the other one, covered by the black plastic bag would be safe from damage. To keep warm we decided to put on our shoes before walking through the frosty grass. That only took a few minutes, but while we were doing up our laces we heard a lot of barking and snarling. Looking out of the window we saw Wags in a frenzy attacking the tree covered with the black plastic bag. He hadn't seen Val covering the tree and now had discovered something different in his garden. That meant 'Attack!'.

He hurled himself at the bag and the small tree underneath it, and before we could get outside he had ripped the bag to shreds and almost pulled the tree out of the ground. Our Wags is very courageous in attacking plastic bags and other things that don't fight back. The damage was so bad that I suggested digging the trees out and starting again. However, Val simply pruned both trees back to make small stumps and, lo and behold, they both produced new shoots and now we have two attractive shrubs bearing hundreds of small flowers. Out of what appeared to be dead and useless stumps new trees grew. This proved that Job knew what he was talking about when he said,

> For there is hope for a tree,
> If it is cut down, that it will sprout again,
> And that its tender shoots will not cease

(Job 14:7).

Our text and reading describe Christ as being a 'Branch' that would grow out of what appeared to be a dead family tree. Christ's ancestor, Jesse, from whom King David descended, was a faithful, godly man. However, over the years the kingdom of Israel collapsed and Jesse's descendants were not recognized as being of princely stock. Joseph and Mary, both descendants of the royal house, were very poor people. The prophet Amos wrote of David's descendant who would again become great:

On that day I will raise up
The tabernacle of David, which has fallen down,
And repair its damages

(Amos 9:11).

Yes, the stump of Jesse appeared dead and useless. His descendants had no power at all. It was when man could do nothing that God intervened, and the stump sprouted forth a 'Branch' — the Lord Jesus Christ — who would bear much fruit.

As you read through today's reading I hope that you recognized that the words referred to Christ, the Son of God. The Spirit of God would come upon him to fully equip him for the redeeming task he was to fulfil. The 'Branch' would be all-wise. He would be a great 'counsellor' having 'might'. He would have a fear and knowledge of the Lord as well as exercising righteous judgement in his dealings with people. His character would be marked with humility. These characteristics would make 'the Branch' a glorious ruler who would establish a kingdom of peace and tranquillity for people from all parts of the world — not just the Jews.

We have seen the truth of Isaiah's words fulfilled in the Lord Jesus Christ. His kingdom is one of peace with God and peace between its members. Our salvation was perfectly planned and accomplished because God is almighty. As we read the Scriptures we discover wise counsel, for we find there the invitation to turn to Christ and trust him for eternal life. The 'Branch' of Isaiah 11 is my Saviour. Is he yours?

To think about

1. Find out all you can about Jesse and his family (Read 1 Samuel 16 and 1 Chronicles 2:12-17).
2. Our reading speaks of the leopard lying down with the young goat. What does this mean to you?
3. What does verse 9 tell you about heaven?
4. Are you a Christian? How do you know?

If you have read this book why not send a postcard of your homeland to me at the following address?

Jim Cromarty
3 Appaloosa Place
Wingham
NSW 2429
Australia